Bootstrap for AS

Incorporate Bootstrap into your ASP.NET MVC projects and make your websites more user friendly and dynamic

Pieter van der Westhuizen

[PACKT] PUBLISHING open source community experience distilled

BIRMINGHAM - MUMBAI

Bootstrap for ASP.NET MVC

First published: August 2014

Production reference: 1130814

Published by Packt Publishing Ltd.
Livery Place
35 Livery Street
Birmingham B3 2PB, UK.

ISBN 978-1-78398-728-3

www.packtpub.com

Cover image by Bartosz Chucherko (chucherko@gmx.com)

Credits

Author
Pieter van der Westhuizen

Reviewers
Jaco Fouché
Tinus Smit
Stephan Swart

Commissioning Editor
Amarabha Banerjee

Acquisition Editor
Rebecca Youé

Content Development Editor
Priyanka S

Technical Editor
Mrunal Chavan

Copy Editors
Janbal Dharmaraj
Deepa Nambiar
Karuna Narayanan
Alfida Paiva

Project Coordinator
Kartik Vedam

Proofreaders
Bridget Braund
Paul Hindle

Indexer
Hemangini Bari

Production Coordinators
Conidon Miranda
Nilesh R. Mohite
Nitesh Thakur

Cover Work
Nitesh Thakur

About the Author

Pieter van der Westhuizen is a freelance software and web developer specializing in ASP.NET MVC, web technologies, and MS Office development. He started his career in web development using classic ASP, Visual InterDev, HoTMetaL, and FrontPage.

Pieter has over 15 years of experience in the IT industry and is also one of the people fortunate enough to have his hobby become his full-time profession. He is also a technology evangelist for Add-in Express (`www.add-in-express.com`), which focuses on tools for Microsoft Office integration.

This is Pieter's first foray into book writing although he has been blogging since 2007 on his personal blog at `www.mythicalmanmoth.com` and on the Add-in Express blog since 2010. He lives with his wife and Harrier (the dog, not the bird or Jump Jet) in Pretoria, South Africa.

Acknowledgments

To everyone who contributed to this book, thank you! A big thanks to the team at Packt Publishing, especially Rebecca, Priyanka, Kartik, and Aboli, for their guidance, advice, and professionalism.

Thanks to my three technical reviewers, Jaco, Tinus, and Stephan, for patiently reading each chapter, reviewing each line of code, and contributing suggestions. You helped shape this book into what it is.

I'd like to express my greatest love and gratitude towards my wife, Andrea, for all her support, impromptu editing sessions, being a soundboard for brainstorming sessions, and the general motivational pep talks during the writing of this book.

To my parents—even though they were not exactly sure what this book was about—thank you for all your support and for allowing me to tinker with the family computer from an early age.

I'd also like to extend a special thank you to Eugene Starostin from Add-in Express, who allowed me to blog about an idea that subsequently turned into this book.

About the Reviewers

Jaco Fouché has been involved with software development for over 22 years and is currently a database architect and software developer at SilverBridge in Pretoria, South Africa. He holds a B.Sc degree in Computer Science from the University of Pretoria. He has worked with different technologies but specializes in Microsoft technologies with specific emphasis on ASP.NET MVC and Microsoft SQL Server.

With a number of years in the coding field, **Tinus Smit** has a passion for good, clean code and solving problems. A C# .NET developer at his core, he has also gained extensive knowledge of Microsoft SQL, Microsoft Dynamics CRM, JavaScript, Entity Framework, and MVC.

The CRM experience is not limited to clicking a few buttons and dragging fields around in a form. He has had a hand in solving complex business problems with CRM's workflow and plugin engines, often integrating with other systems in the process. Over the years, he has learned exactly where CRM fits best, what the product can do, where and how to extend it, and the best practices thereof.

However, in the end, these are merely tools to solve problems. In Johannesburg, South Africa, he finds himself working tirelessly on projects for many companies over the years (from small to enterprise-sized), using these tools and experience. He sees every new challenge as an opportunity to learn something new and finds ways to teach what he has learned. Armed with a database and Visual Studio, he uses pragmatism and logic to help users reach their goal.

He can be reached on Twitter at `@CodingWithTinus` or on his blog at `http://codingwithtinus.wordpress.com`.

Stephan Swart has been interested in software development for the last 30 years. He has used a variety of technologies, programming languages, and platforms. Starting as a Cobol developer, embracing most of the latest technologies that were released at the time, he has been involved in .NET development since the very first release of .NET. In the last few years, he has lived and worked as a senior .NET developer using Web, Windows, and mobile technologies for a number of different companies in Europe, Canada, and South Africa. Among the technologies he used recently are ASP.NET MVC, jQuery, Knockout, C#, VB .NET, WPF, Silverlight, MVVM, Xamarin, and many more.

www.PacktPub.com

Support files, eBooks, discount offers, and more

You might want to visit www.PacktPub.com for support files and downloads related to your book.

Did you know that Packt offers eBook versions of every book published, with PDF and ePub files available? You can upgrade to the eBook version at www.PacktPub.com and as a print book customer, you are entitled to a discount on the eBook copy. Get in touch with us at service@packtpub.com for more details.

At www.PacktPub.com, you can also read a collection of free technical articles, sign up for a range of free newsletters and receive exclusive discounts and offers on Packt books and eBooks.

PACKTLiB™

http://PacktLib.PacktPub.com

Do you need instant solutions to your IT questions? PacktLib is Packt's online digital book library. Here, you can access, read and search across Packt's entire library of books.

Why subscribe?

- Fully searchable across every book published by Packt
- Copy and paste, print and bookmark content
- On demand and accessible via web browser

Free access for Packt account holders

If you have an account with Packt at www.PacktPub.com, you can use this to access PacktLib today and view nine entirely free books. Simply use your login credentials for immediate access.

Table of Contents

Preface

Twitter Bootstrap, simply known as Bootstrap, is the leading open source CSS/HTML and JavaScript framework on the Internet. Shortly after its launch, it became the most popular project on GitHub. It became so popular that Microsoft announced at their Build 2013 conference that all the web app project templates in Visual Studio 2013 will use Twitter Bootstrap by default.

One of the main reasons why Bootstrap is so prevalent is that it allows developers, many of whom are notoriously bad at user interface design, to build aesthetically pleasant-looking sites with a relatively small amount of effort. Bootstrap also offers a rich ecosystem of free and commercial templates, third-party components, tools, and an active and helpful community.

Using CSS frameworks and Bootstrap in particular with ASP.NET MVC is a natural fit. Bootstrap takes care of the typography, form layouts, and user interface components, and allows the developer to focus on what they are good at, that is, writing code. This aspect is particularly valuable for smaller development companies that do not necessarily have an in-house designer. Bootstrap Version 3 introduced a mobile-first approach, meaning all sites built with Bootstrap will be automatically responsive and optimized to be displayed on devices with smaller screens.

What this book covers

Bootstrap for ASP.NET MVC walks you through the process of creating a fully functioning ASP.NET MVC website, using Bootstrap for its layout and user interface.

Chapter 1, Getting Started with ASP.NET MVC and Bootstrap, focuses on getting started with Bootstrap, from where to get the files, how to include them in your project, and takes a closer look at the default ASP.NET MVC project template. We'll also look at the benefits of bundling and minification of CSS and JavaScript.

Chapter 2, Using Bootstrap CSS and HTML Elements, examines the various Bootstrap CSS and HTML elements, how to include them in your ASP.NET MVC project, and how to configure and use their various options.

Chapter 3, Using Bootstrap Components, will be building on what we've learned in *Chapter 2, Using Bootstrap CSS and HTML Elements*. This chapter scrutinizes the different components such as navigation, alerts, progress bars, button groups, and badges.

Chapter 4, Using Bootstrap JavaScript Plugins, illustrates the use of Bootstrap's JavaScript plugins. We will be experimenting with modal dialogs, contextual dropdowns, tooltips, buttons, and UI components such as accordion and carousel.

Chapter 5, Creating ASP.NET MVC Bootstrap Helpers, guides you through the process of reducing the amount of HTML needed to generate Bootstrap elements by creating ASP.NET MVC helper methods and classes.

Chapter 6, Creating T4 Templates to Scaffold Bootstrap Views, moves on to the more advanced topic of creating T4 templates in order to generate Bootstrap-themed scaffolded views.

Chapter 7, Converting a Bootstrap HTML Template into a Usable ASP.NET MVC Project, shows how we can convert an open source HTML template and make it ready to be used with ASP.NET MVC.

Chapter 8, Using the jQuery DataTables Plugin with Bootstrap, demonstrates how to use the powerful jQuery DataTables plugin with Bootstrap and ASP.NET in order to show tabular data.

Chapter 9, Making Things Easier with the TwitterBootstrapMVC Library, examines the TwitterBootstrapMVC library, which contains a host of prebuilt HTML helpers to make the inclusion of Bootstrap components in ASP.NET MVC easier.

Appendix, Bootstrap Resources, provides a list of free Bootstrap resources, themes, and tools.

What you need for this book

To get the most out of this book, you'll need Visual Studio 2013 and a modern browser. All examples have been tested with Visual Studio 2013, Google Chrome, and Mozilla Firefox. This book will be beneficial to those with experience ranging from the entry level to the advanced level in ASP.NET MVC development, as well as limited experience in Bootstrap.

Who this book is for

This book is for ASP.NET MVC developers who would like to know how to incorporate Bootstrap into their projects. ASP.NET MVC developers could also benefit from the chapters that cover advanced topics, such as creating helpers and using the jQuery DataTables plugin. If you have limited experience in ASP.NET MVC and Bootstrap, this book can serve as a primer to these technologies.

Conventions

In this book, you will find a number of styles of text that distinguish between different kinds of information. Here are some examples of these styles, and an explanation of their meaning.

Code words in text, database table names, folder names, filenames, file extensions, pathnames, dummy URLs, user input, and Twitter handles are shown as follows: "We would only need to include the `bootstrap.css` file into our project for the Bootstrap styles to be applied to our pages."

A block of code is set as follows:

```
<system.web>
  <compilation debug="true" targetFramework="4.5" />
  <httpRuntime targetFramework="4.5" />
</system.web>
```

When we wish to draw your attention to a particular part of a code block, the relevant lines or items are set in bold:

```
<script src="https://ajax.googleapis.com/ajax/libs/jquery/1.11.0/
jquery.min.js"></script>
<script src="/bootstrap/js?v=raqa-So7giLQpXYq5LQiW8D-
yNoxOAJewB8VXtgFHfE1"></script>
</body>
</html>
```

Any command-line input or output is written as follows:

```
Install-Package jquery.datatables
```

New terms and **important words** are shown in bold. Words that you see on the screen, in menus or dialog boxes for example, appear in the text like this: "Right-click on the `Controller` folder in the **Solution Explorer** section and navigate to **Add** | **Controller...**."

[Warnings or important notes appear in a box like this.]

[Tips and tricks appear like this.]

Reader feedback

Feedback from our readers is always welcome. Let us know what you think about this book—what you liked or may have disliked. Reader feedback is important for us to develop titles that you really get the most out of.

To send us general feedback, simply send an e-mail to `feedback@packtpub.com`, and mention the book title through the subject of your message.

If there is a topic that you have expertise in and you are interested in either writing or contributing to a book, see our author guide on `www.packtpub.com/authors`.

Customer support

Now that you are the proud owner of a Packt book, we have a number of things to help you to get the most from your purchase.

Downloading the example code

You can download the example code files for all Packt books you have purchased from your account at `http://www.packtpub.com`. If you purchased this book elsewhere, you can visit `http://www.packtpub.com/support` and register to have the files e-mailed directly to you.

Errata

Although we have taken every care to ensure the accuracy of our content, mistakes do happen. If you find a mistake in one of our books—maybe a mistake in the text or the code—we would be grateful if you would report this to us. By doing so, you can save other readers from frustration and help us improve subsequent versions of this book. If you find any errata, please report them by visiting `http://www.packtpub.com/support`, selecting your book, clicking on the **errata submission form** link, and entering the details of your errata. Once your errata are verified, your submission will be accepted and the errata will be uploaded to our website, or added to any list of existing errata, under the Errata section of that title.

Piracy

Piracy of copyright material on the Internet is an ongoing problem across all media. At Packt, we take the protection of our copyright and licenses very seriously. If you come across any illegal copies of our works, in any form, on the Internet, please provide us with the location address or website name immediately so that we can pursue a remedy.

Please contact us at `copyright@packtpub.com` with a link to the suspected pirated material.

We appreciate your help in protecting our authors, and our ability to bring you valuable content.

Questions

You can contact us at `questions@packtpub.com` if you are having a problem with any aspect of the book, and we will do our best to address it.

1
Getting Started with ASP.NET MVC and Bootstrap

As developers, we can find it difficult to create great-looking user interfaces from scratch when using HTML and CSS. This is especially hard when developers have years of developing Windows Forms applications experience. Microsoft introduced Web Forms to abstract the complexities of building websites away for Windows Forms developers and to ease the switch from Windows Forms to the Web, this in turn made it very hard for Web Forms developers to switch to ASP.NET MVC and even harder for Windows Forms developers.

Twitter Bootstrap is a set of stylized components, plugins, and a layout grid that takes care of the heavy lifting. Microsoft included Bootstrap in all ASP.NET MVC project templates since 2013. In the sample project, we'll start by creating a new ASP.NET MVC project either by using the standard Visual Studio MVC project template or by starting with an empty MVC project and adding the necessary files as we need them.

In this chapter, we will cover the following topics:

- The files included in the Bootstrap distribution
- How to create an ASP.NET MVC site using the standard Visual Studio project template and Bootstrap
- How to create an empty ASP.NET MVC site and add the Bootstrap files manually
- How to create a `Layout` file that references the Bootstrap files
- Adding Bootstrap files using NuGet
- Improving site performance with bundling and minification

The Bootstrap distribution

Before we can get started with Bootstrap, we first need to download its source files. At the time of writing this book, Bootstrap was at Version 3.1.1. You can download the latest version from `http://getbootstrap.com`.

The zip archive contains the following three folders:

- `css`
- `fonts`
- `js`

Bootstrap style sheets (the css folder)

Do not be alarmed with the amount of files inside the `css` folder. This folder contains four `.css` files and two `.map` files. We would only need to include the `bootstrap.css` file in our project for the Bootstrap styles to be applied to our pages. The `bootstrap.min.css` file is simply a minified version of the aforementioned file.

The `.map` files can be ignored for the project we'll be creating. These files are used as a type of debug symbol (similar to the `.pdb` files in Visual Studio), which allow developers to live edit their preprocessor source files—something which is beyond the scope of this book.

Bootstrap fonts (the fonts folder)

Bootstrap uses **Font Awesome** to display various icons and glyphs in Bootstrap sites. Font Awesome was designed specifically for Bootstrap and the `fonts` folder contains the following four different formats of the font files:

- Embedded OpenType (`glyphicons-halflings-regular.eot`)
- Scalable Vector Graphics (`glyphicons-halflings-regular.svg`)
- TrueType font (`glyphicons-halflings-regular.ttf`)
- Web Open Font Format (`glyphicons-halflings-regular.woff`)

It is a good idea to include all these files in your web project as this will enable your site to display the fonts correctly in different browsers.

> The EOT font format is required for Internet Explorer 9 and newer. TTF is the traditional old font format and WOFF is a compressed form of TTF fonts. If you only need to support Internet Explorer 8 and later, iOS 4 and higher, as well as Android, you will only need to include the WOFF font.

Bootstrap JavaScript files (the js folder)

The `js` folder contains two files. All the Bootstrap plugins are contained in the `bootstrap.js` file. The `bootstrap.min.js` file is simply a minified version of the aforementioned file. Before including the file in your project, make sure that you have a reference to the jQuery library because all Bootstrap plugins require jQuery.

The default project template automatically adds the jQuery library to your project and creates a bundle for it. The jQuery bundle will be included in your pages if you have the following line of code inside your view:

```
@Scripts.Render("~/bundles/jquery")
```

> **Downloading the example code**
>
> You can download the example code files for all Packt books you have purchased from your account at `http://www.packtpub.com`. If you purchased this book elsewhere, you can visit `http://www.packtpub.com/support` and register to have the files e-mailed directly to you.

The Bootstrap folder structure

The unzipped folder structure for Bootstrap will look something like the following screenshot:

```
bootstrap/
├── css/
│   ├── bootstrap.css
│   ├── bootstrap.min.css
│   ├── bootstrap-theme.css
│   └── bootstrap-theme.min.css
├── js/
│   ├── bootstrap.js
│   └── bootstrap.min.js
└── fonts/
    ├── glyphicons-halflings-regular.eot
    ├── glyphicons-halflings-regular.svg
    ├── glyphicons-halflings-regular.ttf
    └── glyphicons-halflings-regular.woff
```

Using Bootstrap with a site created with the standard Visual Studio project template

From Visual Studio 2013, when creating an ASP.NET project, you only have one project template to choose from, that is, the ASP.NET Web Application project template, as shown in the following screenshot:

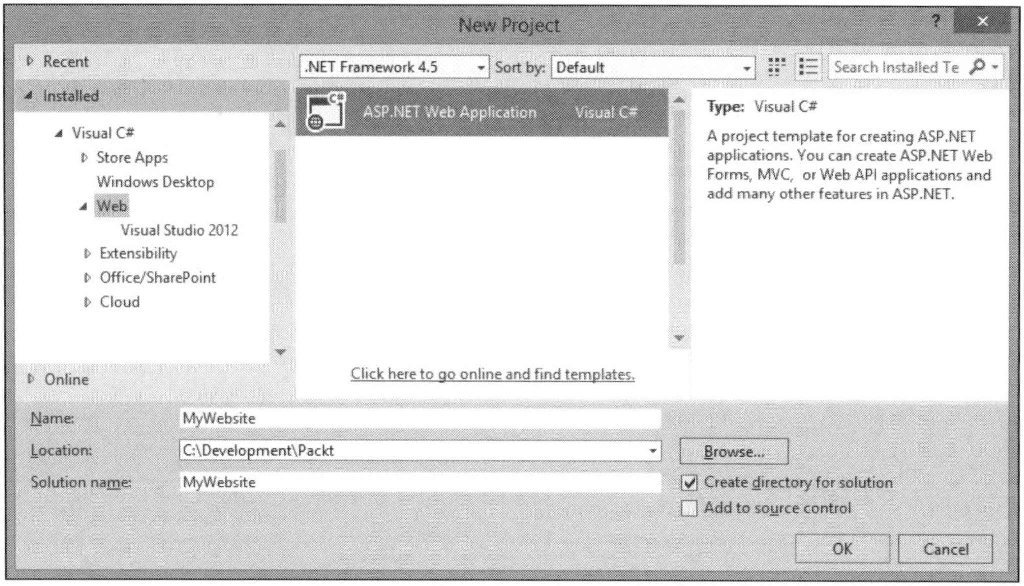

In the **New ASP.NET Project** dialog, you have a choice to select the type of ASP.NET web application you would like to create. To create an ASP.NET MVC web app that uses Bootstrap for its styling and layout, select the **MVC** template. You'll notice that the **MVC** checkbox is automatically selected, as shown in the following screenshot:

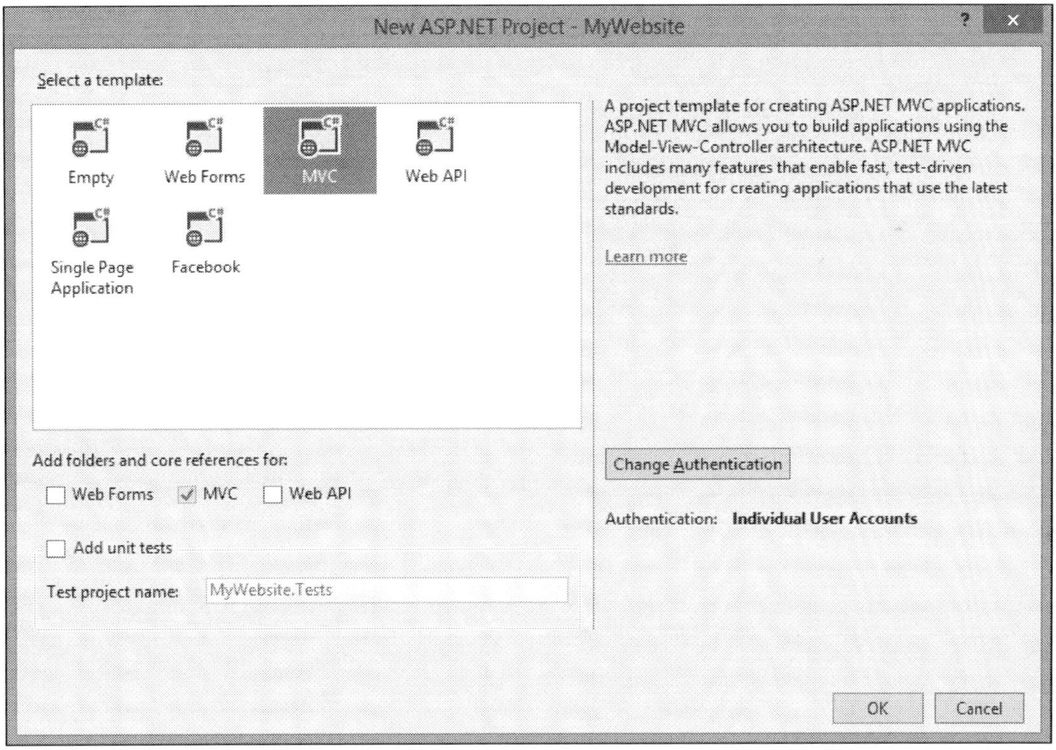

Click on the **OK** button to finish the creation of the MVC project in Visual Studio. You'll notice that the project template automatically adds a number of NuGet packages to your project, including the Bootstrap NuGet package.

Examining the default MVC project layout

The default project template adds all the necessary Bootstrap files we discussed earlier, although it does not use the same folder naming convention as the default Bootstrap distribution. The default project layout will look similar to the following screenshot:

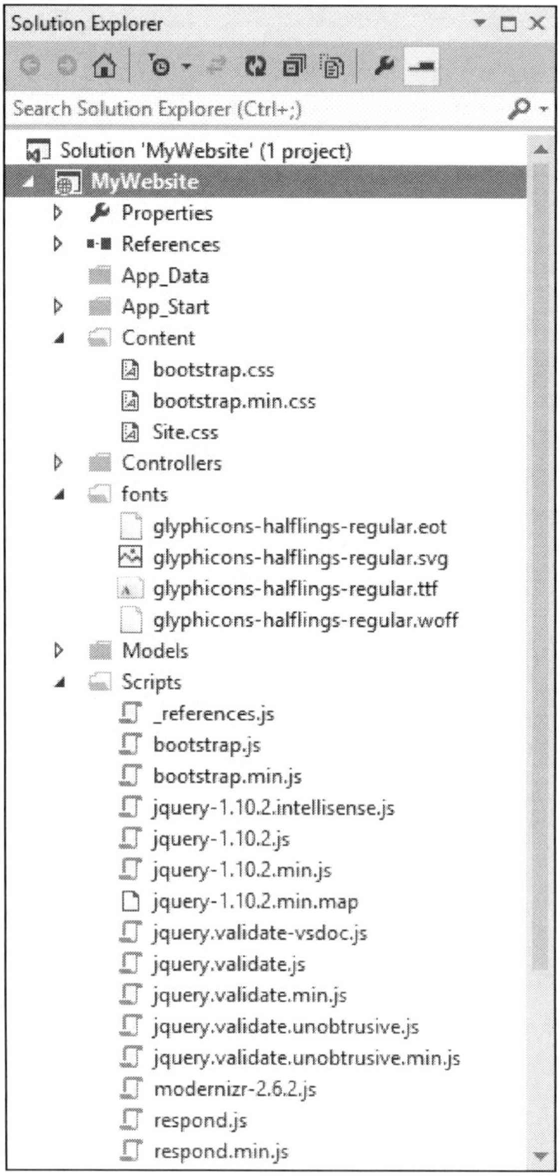

The Content folder

The `Content` folder contains both the `bootstrap.css` and `bootstrap.min.css` files as well as a style sheet called `Site.css`. This file is used to apply any additional styling on top of the default styles provided by Bootstrap, and it is also used to specify the styles to use for the jQuery validation plugin required by ASP.NET MVC for form validation. For example, the following CSS highlights any input element with a reddish color and draws a border around the element if the validation for that field failed:

```
.field-validation-error {
    color: #b94a48;
}

.field-validation-valid {
    display: none;
}

input.input-validation-error {
    border: 1px solid #b94a48;
}

input[type="checkbox"].input-validation-error {
    border: 0 none;
}

.validation-summary-errors {
    color: #b94a48;
}

.validation-summary-valid {
    display: none;
}
```

The fonts folder

The `fonts` folder contains the Glyphicon font in all the necessary formats.

The Scripts folder

The `Scripts` folder contains a number of scripts. Most notably for this book, it contains the `bootstrap.js` and `bootstrap.min.js` JavaScript files. The default ASP.NET MVC project template also adds both minified and normal files for the following JavaScript libraries and plugins:

- jQuery
- jQuery validation plugin
- jQuery and jQuery validation support library for unobtrusive validation
- Modernizr
- Respond JS

Visual Studio enables intelliSense for jQuery, Bootstrap, and Modernizr as well as responds by adding the `_reference.js` file to the `Scripts` folder. This is a very useful feature when working with JavaScript and well worth using when working with the Bootstrap components.

Most of these libraries and files are beyond the scope of this book, but we will touch on some of them as we progress.

Creating an empty ASP.NET MVC site and adding Bootstrap manually

The default project layout is a good start for any ASP.NET MVC project, but for the sample project we'll be building throughout this book, we'll create an empty ASP.NET MVC site and add the necessary files manually. This is done by performing the following steps:

1. Start by creating a new ASP.NET web application project in Visual Studio and name the project `Northwind.Web`.
2. This time, select the **Empty** template in the **New ASP.NET Project** dialog and make sure the **MVC** checkbox is selected, as shown in the following screenshot:

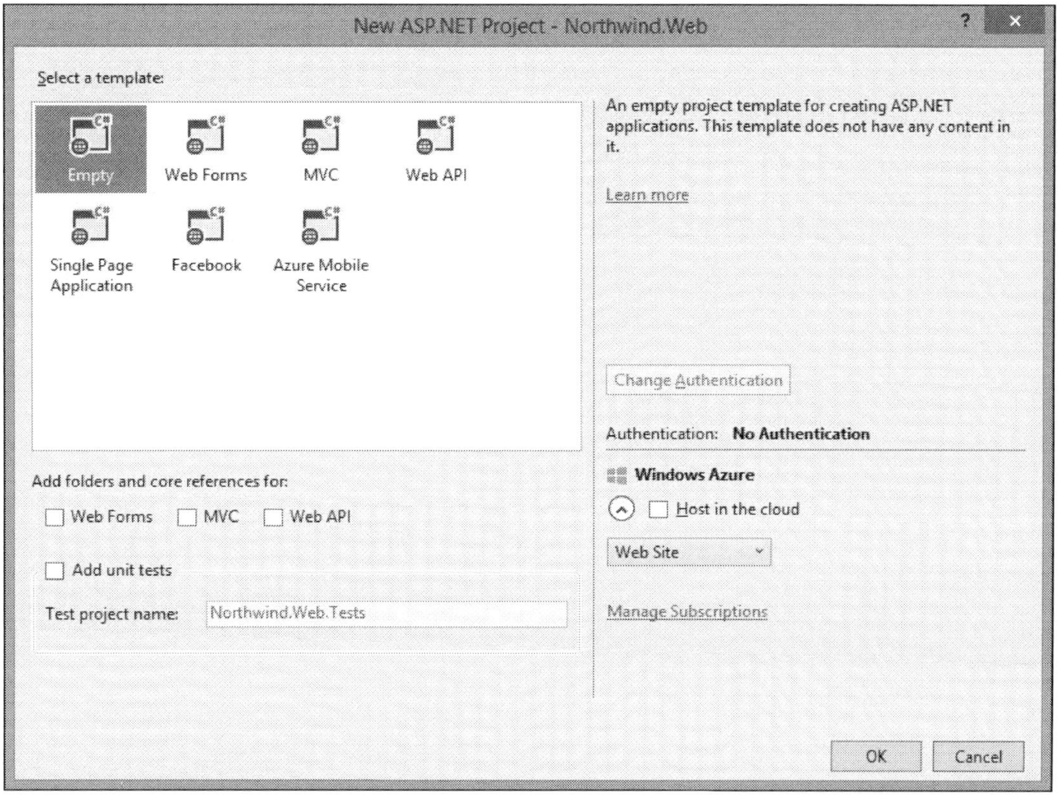

3. An empty project layout will be created for you and you'll notice that we do not have the `Content`, `Fonts`, or `Scripts` folder—we'll add them ourselves!

Adding the Bootstrap style sheets

To add the Bootstrap style sheet files to your project, complete the following steps:

1. Create a new folder by right-clicking on the new project's name inside Visual Studio's **Solution Explorer** and navigating to **Add | New Folder**, name the new folder `css`.
2. Next, right-click on the newly created `css` folder and navigate to **Add | Existing Item...** from the context menu.
3. Browse to the folder in which you've extracted the Bootstrap distribution files and select the `bootstrap.css` file that you can locate in the `css` folder.

Adding the Bootstrap fonts

Add the required Bootstrap fonts by performing the following steps:

1. As with the style sheets, create a new folder called `fonts`.
2. Next, browse to the location to where you've extracted the Bootstrap download and add all the files from the `fonts` folder to your `fonts` folder in Visual Studio.
3. There should be four files in total, each named `glyphicons-halflings-regular` but with the following different file extensions:
    - `.eot`
    - `.svg`
    - `.ttf`
    - `.woff`

Adding the Bootstrap JavaScript files

The final Bootstrap file we'll need is `bootstrap.js`. To add it, perform the following steps:

1. Before adding the `bootstrap.js` file to your Visual Studio project, create a new folder called `js`.
2. Add the `bootstrap.js` file to this folder.
3. Once completed, the project layout should look similar to the following screenshot in the Visual Studio's **Solution Explorer**:

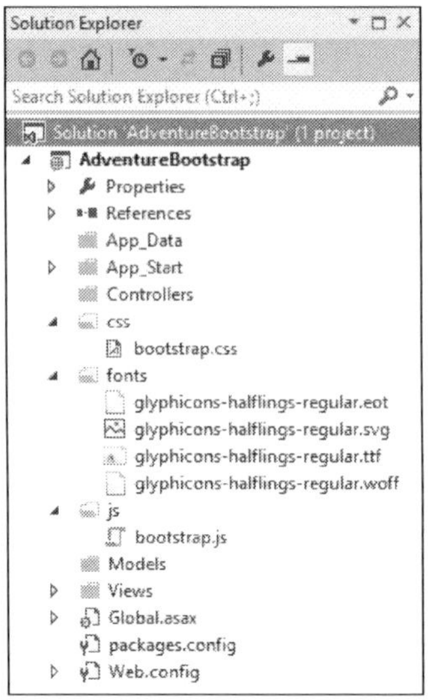

Creating the site Layout file

To maintain a persistent look across our site's pages, we'll use a `Layout` file. This layout file will use the basic Bootstrap HTML template at first and we'll build onto it as we progress throughout the book. To create this file, complete the following steps:

1. Create a new `Layout` file by right-clicking on the `Views` folder in the Visual Studio's **Solution Explorer** and navigate to **Add | New Folder**. Name the new folder `Shared`.
2. Next, right-click on the `Shared` folder and navigate to **Add | New Item...**. Select the **MVC 5 Layout Page (Razor)** item template, name the new item `_Layout.cshtml` and click on **Add**, as shown in the following screenshot:

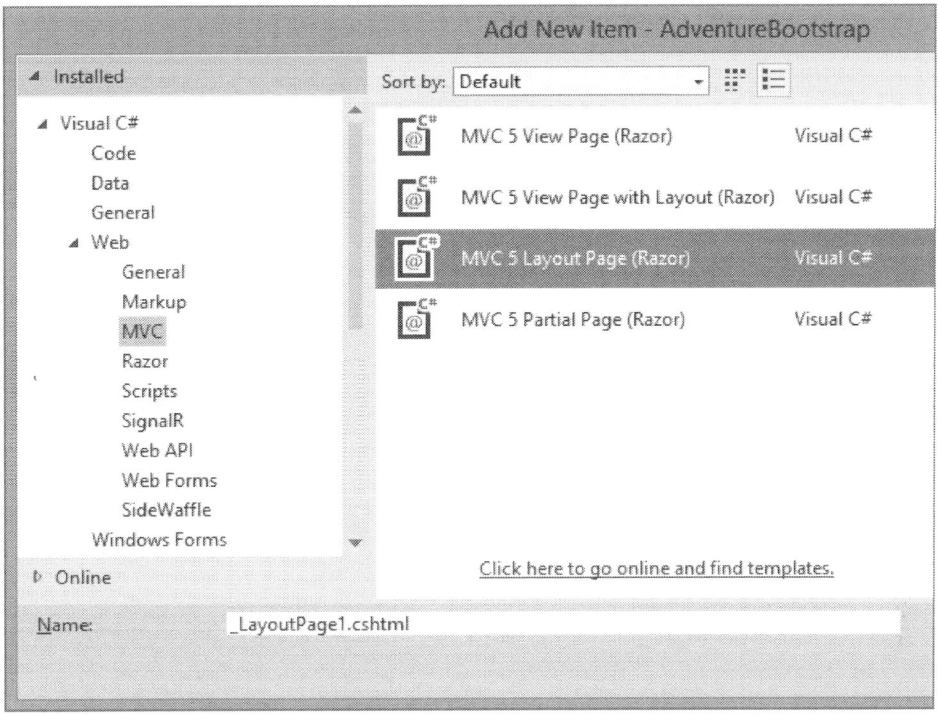

3. After the new file is added to you project, open it and replace its contents with the following HTML markup:

```
<!DOCTYPE html>
<html lang="en">
<head>
    <meta charset="utf-8">
```

```
    <meta http-equiv="X-UA-Compatible" content="IE=edge">
    <meta name="viewport" content="width=device-width,
    initial-scale=1">
    <title>@ViewBag.Title</title>
    <!-- Bootstrap -->
    <link href="@Url.Content("~/css/bootstrap.css")"
    rel="stylesheet">
    <!--[if lt IE 9]>
      <script src="https://oss.maxcdn.com/libs/html5shiv/3.7.0/
      html5shiv.js"></script>
      <script src="https://oss.maxcdn.com/libs/respond.js/1.4.2/
      respond.min.js"></script>
    <![endif]-->
</head>
<body>
    @RenderBody()
    <script src="https://ajax.googleapis.com/ajax/libs/
    jquery/1.11.0/jquery.min.js"></script>
    <script src="@Url.Content("~/js/bootstrap.js")"></script>
</body>
</html>
```

In the preceding markup, we set the viewport's `width` property to the device's width and the `initial-scale` value to `1`. This will cause our site to adapt to the screen size of the device the user is viewing it from.

Next, we reference the Bootstrap style sheet by using the `Url.Content` helper method. This helper method converts a virtual or relative path to an absolute path, making sure that when the web page is opened, the style sheet will be loaded correctly.

We then check if the browser accessing the site is Internet Explorer 9 or earlier; if it is, we include the `HTML5Shiv` workaround that enables styling of HTML5 elements in Internet Explorer Version 9 and earlier. We also include the version of the `Respond JS` library suitable for versions of IE9 and earlier.

Just before the closing the <body> tag of the file, we include the jQuery library and the `bootstrap` JavaScript library.

> Note that the `HTML5Shiv` workaround, Respond JS, and jQuery files are loaded from a **Content Delivery Network (CDN)**. This is a good approach to use when referencing to most of the widely used JavaScript libraries. This should allow your site to load faster if the user has already visited a site, which uses the same library from the same CDN, because the library will be cached in their browser.

Creating a home controller with a Bootstrap-themed view

At the moment, the site we've created will return an error message that states that the requested resource cannot be found, when we run the project. We first need to add a new home controller and associate a view with its default action in order to avoid any errors. To add a new controller, perform the following steps:

1. Right-click on the `Controller` folder in the **Solution Explorer** section and navigate to **Add** | **Controller...**.
2. In the **Add Scaffold** dialog, select the **MVC 5 Controller - Empty** item, as shown in the following screenshot:

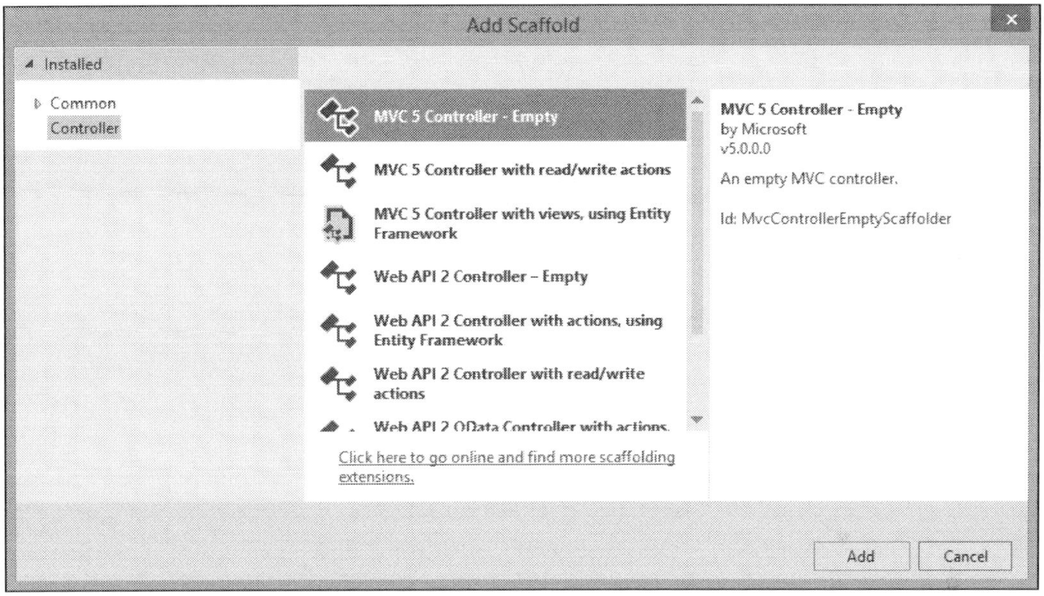

3. When prompted, in the **Add Controller** dialog, enter `HomeController` as the new controller name and click on **Add**.
4. After the controller has been added, right-click inside the empty **Index** method and select **Add View**. The method is considered empty if it has only the one `return View()` statement in it.

5. In the **Add View** dialog, leave all the fields at their default values and select the layout page we've added earlier. Click on **Add** to continue, as shown in the following screenshot:

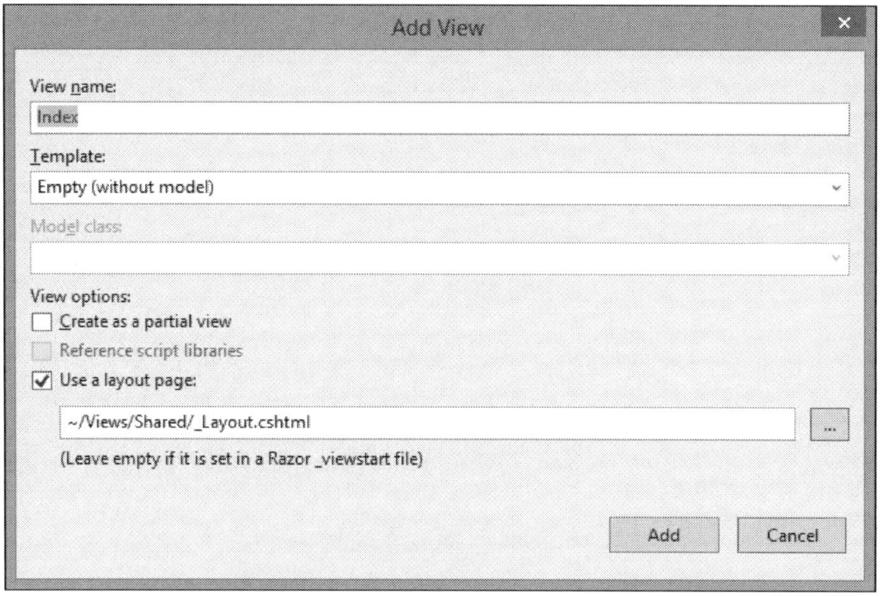

6. An empty view will be generated and you'll notice the `ViewBag.Title` property as well as the layout page to use for this view have been added at the top of the view. Consider the following example:

```
@{
    ViewBag.Title = "Index";
    Layout = "~/Views/Shared/_Layout.cshtml";
}
```

There will also be a single `<h2>` element in the view that you can leave as is. If you run your project, you should see the view displayed with the default Bootstrap styling applied to the `<h2>` element.

Adding Bootstrap files using NuGet

So far we've created two ASP.NET MVC projects that use the Bootstrap frontend framework. The first included the Bootstrap assets by default because we created it with the standard ASP.NET MVC Visual Studio project template. The second, we created an empty ASP.NET MVC project and added the Bootstrap files manually.

NuGet is a package manager for the .NET framework and can be used to automatically add files and references to your Visual Studio projects. A Bootstrap package exists on the NuGet gallery site, which enables you to automatically add the Bootstrap assets to your project.

Bear in mind that though the Bootstrap NuGet package assumes that you want your Bootstrap files in the `Content` and `Scripts` folders and will create the folders and files as such, it will also automatically check whether you have the jQuery library referenced and if not, add it by design.

> NuGet is a package manager for the Microsoft development platform that makes it easy to add references to existing libraries. You can read more about it on `https://www.nuget.org/`.

Adding the Bootstrap NuGet package using the dialog

One option for adding the Bootstrap NuGet package to your project is to use the **Manage NuGet Packages** dialog box. To access the **Manage NuGet Packages** dialog and add the Bootstrap NuGet package, perform the following steps:

1. Right-click on the **References** node in the **Solution Explorer** section and select **Manage NuGet Packages**. Click on the **Online** tab and type `bootstrap` in the search box and press *Enter*, as shown in the following screenshot:

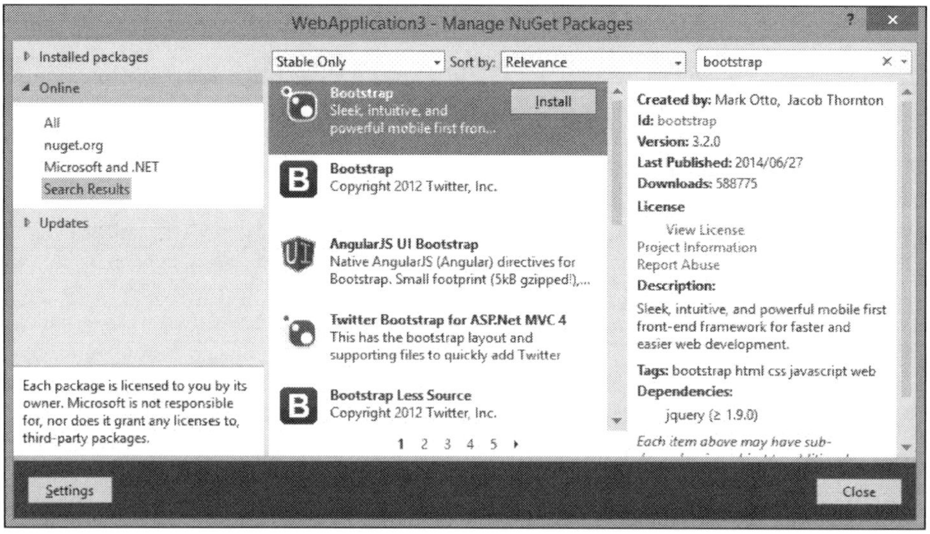

2. Click on the **Install** button to add the Bootstrap files to your project.

Adding the Bootstrap NuGet package using the Package Manager Console

The second method of adding NuGet packages to your Visual Studio project is via the **Package Manager Console** and completing the following steps:

1. Inside Visual Studio, from the **Tools** menu, navigate to **Library Package Manager | Package Manager Console**. This will open the **Package Manager Console** window.
2. To install the Bootstrap NuGet packages, type `Install-Package bootstrap`, as shown in the following screenshot:

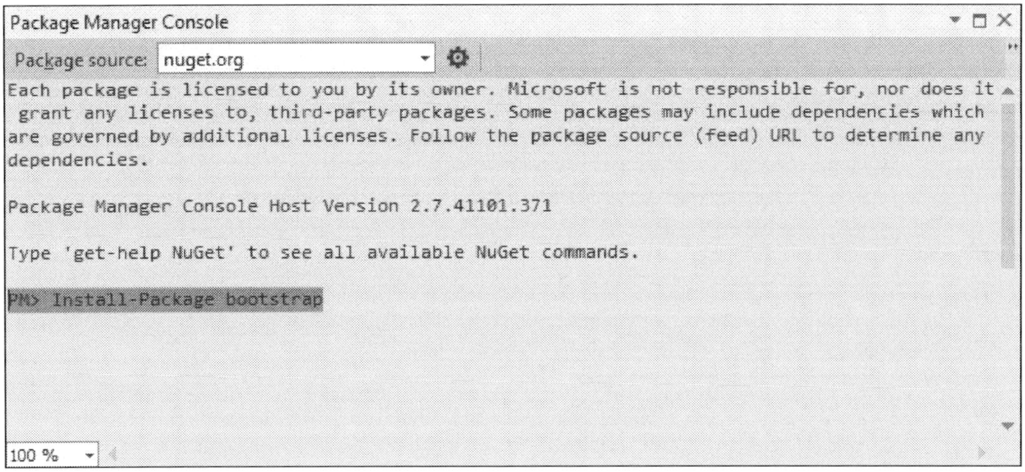

3. This will create the `Content`, `fonts`, and `Scripts` folders and add the necessary Bootstrap files to each.

Improving your site performance with bundling and minification

Bundling and minification is a feature in ASP.NET that allows you to increase the speed at which your site loads. This is accomplished by limiting the number of requests to CSS and JavaScript files your site needs to make by combining these types of files into one large file and removing all unnecessary characters, such as comments, white spaces, and new line characters from the files.

> Most modern browsers have a limit of six concurrent connections per hostname. This means that if you reference more than six CSS or JavaScript files on a page, the browser will only download six files at a time and queue the rest. Limiting the number of CSS and JavaScript files is always a good idea.

Adding bundling to your Bootstrap project

Because we created an empty ASP.NET MVC site, the necessary reference for adding bundling was not automatically added to our project. Luckily, this can easily be added by using the NuGet **Package Manager Console** as follows:

1. Open the **Package Manager Console** window and enter the following command:

   ```
   install-package Microsoft.AspNet.Web.Optimization
   ```

2. This will install the `Microsoft.AspNet.Web.Optimization` NuGet package as well as all the packages it has dependencies on. These dependencies are as follows:
   - `Microsoft.Web.Infrastructure`
   - `WebGrease`
   - `Antlr`
   - `Newtonsoft.Json`

3. After the NuGet packages have been installed successfully, create a new static class called `BundleConfig` inside the `App_Start` folder.

4. Inside this class, we'll create a new static method called `RegisterBundles`, which accepts a parameter called `bundles`, whose type is a `BundleCollection` object. The code for the class is as follows:

   ```
   public class BundleConfig
   {
       public static void RegisterBundles(BundleCollection bundles)
       {
           bundles.Add(new ScriptBundle("~/bootstrap/js").Include(
                   "~/js/bootstrap.js",
                   "~/js/site.js"));

           bundles.Add(new StyleBundle("~/bootstrap/css").Include(
                   "~/css/bootstrap.css",
                   "~/css/site.css"));
       }
   }
   ```

   Bundles come in the following two types:
   - `ScriptBundle`
   - `StyleBundle`

The `StyleBundle` object is used to add style sheets to a bundle and the `ScriptBundle` object is used to add JavaScript files. The `Add` method of the `BundleCollection` object accepts both types of objects. The `StyleBundle` and `ScriptBundle` objects accept a string parameter, which specifies the virtual path of the files, and you should therefore, use the `Include` method to specify the path to the files you would like to include in the bundle.

> Never include files with `.min` in their names, for example, `bootstrap.min.css` or `bootstrap.min.js` in bundles. The compiler will ignore these files as they are already minified.

Including bundles in your ASP.NET layout

To include the bundles we created earlier in our `Layout` file, perform the following steps:

1. Open the `_Layout.cshtml` file in the `Shared` folder and change its markup to reflect the following (changes are highlighted):

```
<!DOCTYPE html>
<html lang="en">
<head>
    <meta charset="utf-8">
    <meta http-equiv="X-UA-Compatible" content="IE=edge">
    <meta name="viewport" content="width=device-width,
    initial-scale=1">
    <title>@ViewBag.Title</title>
    @Styles.Render("~/bootstrap/css")

    <!--[if lt IE 9]>
      <script src="https://oss.maxcdn.com/libs/html5shiv/3.7.0/
      html5shiv.js"></script>
      <script src="https://oss.maxcdn.com/libs/respond.js/1.4.2/
      respond.min.js"></script>
    <![endif]-->
</head>
<body>
    @RenderBody()
    <script src="https://ajax.googleapis.com/ajax/libs/
    jquery/1.11.0/jquery.min.js"></script>
    @Scripts.Render("~/bootstrap/js")
</body>
```

2. If the Visual Studio HTML editor indicates that it cannot find the `Scripts` or `Styles` objects (that is indicated by the words being highlighted), this means a reference is missing from the `Web.config` file inside the `Views` folder.
3. To fix this, add a reference to `System.Web.Optimization` to the list of namespaces in this `Web.config` file. Consider the following example:

```
<namespaces>
  <add namespace="System.Web.Mvc" />
  <add namespace="System.Web.Mvc.Ajax" />
  <add namespace="System.Web.Mvc.Html" />
  <add namespace="System.Web.Routing" />
  <add namespace="AdventureBootstrap" />
  <add namespace="System.Web.Optimization" />
</namespaces>
```

Testing bundling and minification

In order to enable bundling and minification, open the `Web.config` file inside the root of your project and change the `debug` attribute of the `compilation` element to `true` as follows:

```
<system.web>
  <compilation debug="true" targetFramework="4.5" />
  <httpRuntime targetFramework="4.5" />
</system.web>
```

The same can be achieved by setting the `EnableOptimizations` property of the `BundleTable` object to `true`. This statement can either be added to the `Global.asax` file's `Application_Start` method or to the `RegisterBundles` method of the `BundleConfig` class as follows:

```
BundleTable.EnableOptimizations = true;
```

After you've added references to the bundles inside your `Layout` file and set either the `debug` attribute or the `EnableOptimizations` property to `true`, build and run your project. Once the site is open in a browser, view its source. You should see a markup similar to the following:

```
<!DOCTYPE html>
<html lang="en">
<head>
    <meta charset="utf-8">
```

```
    <meta http-equiv="X-UA-Compatible" content="IE=edge">
    <meta name="viewport" content="width=device-width,
    initial-scale=1">
    <title>Index</title>
    <link href="/bootstrap/css?v=Tmmo-oSKW9MFWr7qyt2LfyMD1tap2GokH7
    z1W2bhfgY1" rel="stylesheet"/>
    <!--[if lt IE 9]>
      <script src="https://oss.maxcdn.com/libs/html5shiv/3.7.0/
      html5shiv.js"></script>
      <script src="https://oss.maxcdn.com/libs/respond.js/1.4.2/
      respond.min.js"></script>
    <![endif]-->
</head>
<body>
<h2>Index</h2>
<script src="https://ajax.googleapis.com/ajax/libs/jquery/1.11.0/
jquery.min.js"></script>
<script src="/bootstrap/js?v=raqa-So7giLQpXYq5LQiW8D-
yNoxOAJewB8VXtgFHfE1"></script>
</body>
</html>
```

Note that the highlighted lines contain the relative paths we've specified in our bundles and when clicking on, for example, the `/bootstrap/js` link, the browser will open a minified version of the Bootstrap JavaScript file. You can see it is minified because most white spaces and line breaks have been removed. The code will also be a combination of the Bootstrap JavaScript file as well as any other JavaScript files, which we might have added to the bundle.

Summary

In this chapter, you've learned what is inside the Bootstrap download and how to include these files in your own ASP.NET MVC projects. We've also covered the various techniques of how to include these files and how to increase the performance of your site using bundling and minification.

In the next chapter, we'll dive into the inner working of Bootstrap's CSS and HTML elements and how to use them to design the layout of your site.

2

Using Bootstrap CSS and HTML Elements

Bootstrap provides a wide range of HTML elements and CSS settings as well as an advanced grid system to aid in laying out your web page designs. These settings and elements include utilities to assist with typography, code formatting, table, and form layouts to name a few.

All CSS settings and HTML elements combined with the mobile-first, a fluid grid system, enables developers to build intuitive web interfaces quickly and easily without having to worry about the nuts and bolts of enabling responsiveness for smaller device screens and styling user interface elements.

In this chapter, we will cover the following topics:

- The Bootstrap grid system
- Bootstrap tables and buttons
- Laying out different Bootstrap forms
- Using Bootstrap's validation styles for form validation
- Using editor templates to control the HTML output for form elements
- Using images in Bootstrap and configuring the images to be responsive

The Bootstrap grid system

Many websites are reporting an increasing amount of mobile traffic and this trend is expected to increase over the coming years. The Bootstrap grid system is mobile-first, which means it is designed to target devices with smaller displays and then grow as the display size increases.

Fortunately, this is not something you need to be too concerned about as Bootstrap takes care of most of the heavy lifting.

Bootstrap grid options

Bootstrap 3 introduced a number of predefined grid classes in order to specify the sizes of columns in your design. These class names are listed in the following table:

Class name	Type of device	Resolution	Container width	Column width
`col-xs-*`	Phones	Less than 768 px	Auto	Auto
`col-sm-*`	Tablets	Larger than 768 px	750 px	60 px
`col-md-*`	Desktops	Larger than 992 px	970 px	1170 px
`col-lg-*`	High-resolution desktops	Larger than 1200 px	78 px	95 px

The Bootstrap grid is divided into 12 columns. When laying out your web page, keep in mind that all columns combined should be a total of 12. To illustrate this, consider the following HTML code:

```
<div class="container">
    <div class="row">
    <div class="col-md-3" style="background-color:green;">
            <h3>green</h3>
        </div>
        <div class="col-md-6" style="background-color:red;">
            <h3>red</h3>
        </div>
      <div class="col-md-3" style="background-color:blue;">
            <h3>blue</h3>
        </div>
    </div>
</div>
```

In the preceding code, we have a <div> element, container, with one child <div> element, row. The row div element in turn has three columns. You will notice that two of the columns have a class name of col-md-3 and one of the columns has a class name of col-md-6. When combined, they add up to 12.

The preceding code will work well on all devices with a resolution of 992 pixels or higher. To preserve the preceding layout on devices with smaller resolutions, you'll need to combine the various CSS grid classes. For example, to allow our layout to work on tablets, phones, and medium-sized desktop displays, change the HTML to the following code:

```
<div class="container">
    <div class="row">
    <div class="col-xs-3 col-sm-3 col-md-3" style="background-
    color:green;">
            <h3>green</h3>
        </div>
        <div class="col-xs-6 col-sm-6 col-md-6" style="background-
    color:red;">
            <h3>red</h3>
        </div>
      <div class="col-xs-3 col-sm-3 col-md-3" style="background-
    color:blue;">
            <h3>blue</h3>
        </div>
    </div>
</div>
```

By adding the col-xs-* and col-sm-* class names to the div elements, we'll ensure that our layout will appear the same in a wide range of device resolutions.

Bootstrap HTML elements

Bootstrap provides a host of different HTML elements that are styled and ready to use. These elements include the following:

- Tables
- Buttons
- Forms
- Images

Bootstrap tables

Bootstrap provides a default styling for HTML tables with a few options to customize their layout and behaviors. The default ASP.NET MVC scaffolding automatically adds the `table` class names to the `table` element when generating a list view.

To see this in action, complete the following steps:

1. Create a new view model class in our project's `Models` folder called `ProductViewModel.cs`. This class will contain six properties and its code is listed as follows:

   ```
   public class ProductViewModel
   {
       public int ProductID { get; set; }
       public string ProductName { get; set; }
       public decimal? UnitPrice { get; set; }
       public int? UnitsInStock { get; set; }
       public bool Discontinued { get; set; }
       public string Status { get; set; }
   }
   ```

2. Next, we'll add a new empty `ProductsController` class and only add one action result called `Index` to it:

   ```
   public class ProductsController : Controller
   {
       private readonly ApplicationDbContext _context;
       private readonly ICurrentUser _currentUser;

       public ProductsController(ApplicationDbContext context,
       ICurrentUser currentUser)
       {
           _context = context;
           _currentUser = currentUser;
       }

       public ActionResult Index()
       {
           var models = _context.Products.Project().
       To<ProductViewModel>().ToArray();
           return View(models);
       }
   }
   ```

The preceding code uses a dependency injection to get a reference to the Entity Framework `DBContext` object. The `Index` method then retrieves a collection of products from the database and maps it to the `ProductViewModel` object using AutoMapper. The list is then passed to the view.

> We're using `StructureMap` to perform our project's dependency injection and inversion of control. We're also using a tool called AutoMapper to automatically map our domain models to our project's view models. Both libraries are available via NuGet, and you can read more about each on their respective websites at `www.structuremap.net` and `www.automapper.org`.

Using AutoMapper, we create a conditional mapping to the `Status` property of the `ProductViewModel` class. If the product is discontinued, we'll set the `Status` property to `danger`; if the `UnitPrice` is more than `50`, the `Status` property is set to `info`; and if the `UnitInStock` property is less than `20`, the `Status` property is set to `warning`. The code that performs this logic looks like the following:

```
Mapper.CreateMap<Product, ProductViewModel>()
     .ForMember(dest => dest.Status,
            opt => opt.MapFrom
            (src => src.Discontinued ? "danger" : src.UnitPrice > 50 ?
"info" : src.UnitsInStock < 20 ? "warning" : ""));
```

To generate a view that includes a Bootstrap table, complete the following steps:

1. Right-click inside the `Index` method and select **Add View...** from the context menu. In the **Add View** dialog window, select **List** from the **Template** drop-down menu and the `ProductViewModel` class from the **Model class** drop-down menu.

2. Click on the **Add** button to create the new view, as shown in the following screenshot:

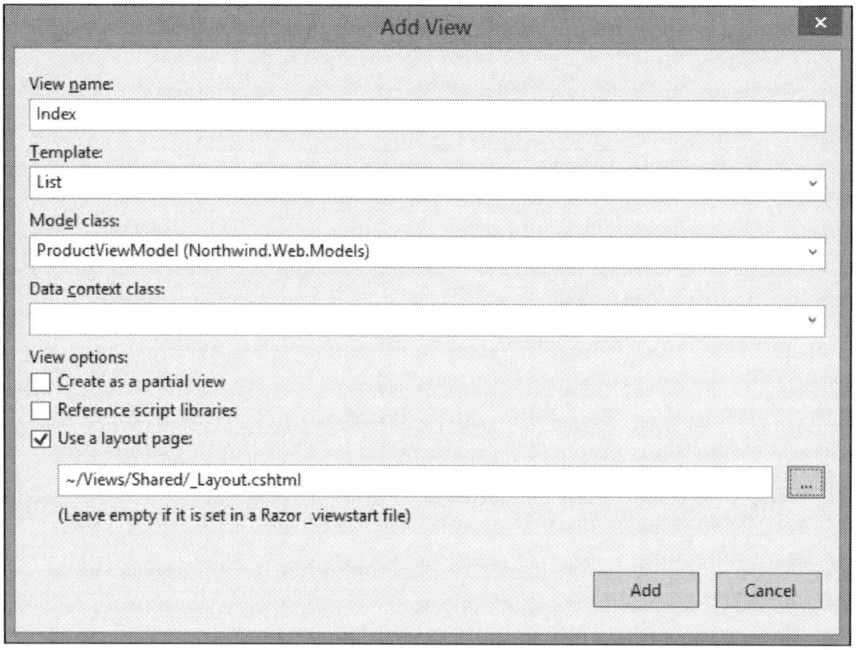

3. The default ASP.NET MVC scaffolding will generate a basic `<table>` element with a class name, `table`. We'll change the default-generated markup by adding a table head element (`<thead>`), which will be used to define the column headings for the table.
4. This element will be followed by a table body element (`<tbody>`). The table body element will contain the actual row data. The resulting markup will look like the following code:

```
<table class="table">
    <thead>
        <tr>
            <th>
                Product Name
            </th>
            <th>
                Unit Price
            </th>
```

```
            <th>
                Units In Stock
            </th>
            <th>
                Discontinued
            </th>
            <th></th>
        </tr>
    </thead>
    <tbody>
        @foreach (var item in Model)
        {
            <tr class="@item.Status">
                <td>
                    @Html.DisplayFor(modelItem => item.
                    ProductName)
                </td>
                <td>
                    @Html.DisplayFor(modelItem => item.UnitPrice)
                </td>
                <td>
                    @Html.DisplayFor(modelItem => item.
                    UnitsInStock)
                </td>
                <td>
                    @Html.DisplayFor(modelItem => item.
                    Discontinued)
                </td>
                <td>
                    @Html.ActionLink("Edit", "Edit", new { /*
                    id=item.PrimaryKey */ }) |
                    @Html.ActionLink("Details", "Details", new {
                    /* id=item.PrimaryKey */ }) |
                    @Html.ActionLink("Delete", "Delete", new { /*
                    id=item.PrimaryKey */ })
                </td>
            </tr>
        }
    </tbody>
</table>
```

In the preceding markup, note that the `<table>` element's class name is set to `table`. When you run the project and open this view, your table should be styled using the Bootstrap table styles as illustrated in the following screenshot:

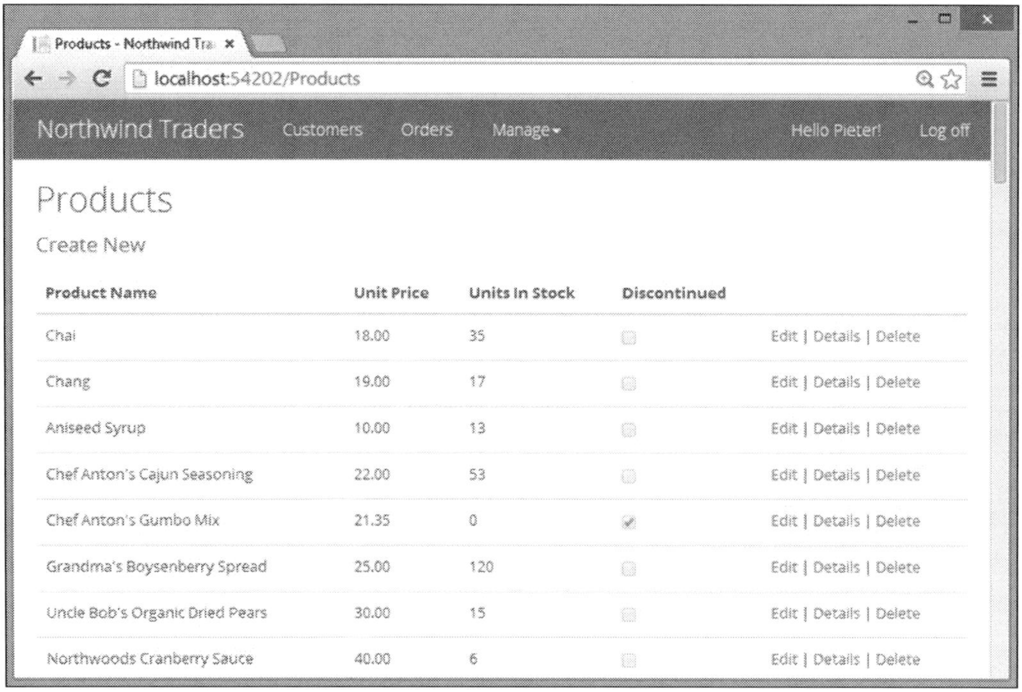

Styling Bootstrap tables

Bootstrap provides additional classes with which you can style your tables even more. To create a bordered table, add `table-bordered` to its class name as follows:

```
<table class="table table-bordered">
```

To create a table where each odd row is highlighted with another color than the base color, change the table's class name to `table table-striped` as follows:

```
<table class="table table-striped">
```

Lastly, Bootstrap also gives you the option to enable the `hover` state on a table. This means the row that the user hovers their cursor over will be highlighted. To accomplish this, change the `table` class to `table table-hover` as follows:

```
<table class="table table-hover">
```

All the different class names can be combined to create a zebra-striped, bordered table with hovering, as illustrated in the following markup:

```
<table class="table table-striped table-bordered table-hover">
```

The result will look similar to the following screenshot in your browser:

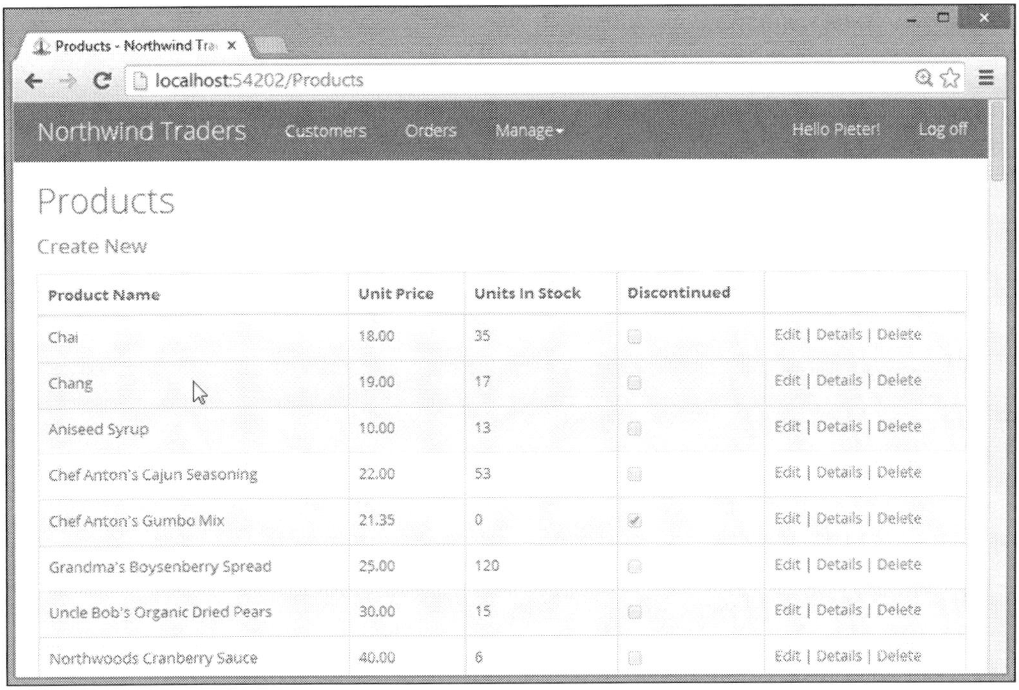

Bootstrap contextual table classes

Bootstrap provides additional classes with which you can style either your table's rows or cells. Adding one of the following classes to either the `<td>` or `<tr>` element of your HTML table will highlight it in either gray, green, blue, orange, or red, which respectively represents the following:

- Active
- Success
- Info
- Warning
- Danger

Of course, we can also apply these styles dynamically in our ASP.NET MVC views. In our `ProductViewModel` view model, we have a `Status` property, which can be one of the five contextual Bootstrap classes. By setting the `<tr>` element's class to this property, we can dynamically change the color of the rows in the table, based on their data as illustrated in the following markup:

```
<tbody>
    @foreach (var item in Model)
    {
        <tr class="@item.Status">
            <td>
                @Html.DisplayFor(modelItem => item.ProductName)
            </td>
            <td>
                @Html.DisplayFor(modelItem => item.UnitPrice)
            </td>
            <td>
                @Html.DisplayFor(modelItem => item.UnitsInStock)
            </td>
            <td>
                @Html.DisplayFor(modelItem => item.Discontinued)
            </td>
            <td>
                @Html.ActionLink("Edit", "Edit", new { /* id=item.
                PrimaryKey */ }) |
                @Html.ActionLink("Details", "Details", new { /*
                id=item.PrimaryKey */ }) |
                @Html.ActionLink("Delete", "Delete", new { /* id=item.
                PrimaryKey */ })
            </td>
        </tr>
    }
</tbody>
```

In the preceding code, you will notice how the table row's class was set to `@item.status`. This will cause the rows to be highlighted based on the mapping we've specified for the `Status` property, as illustrated in the following screenshot:

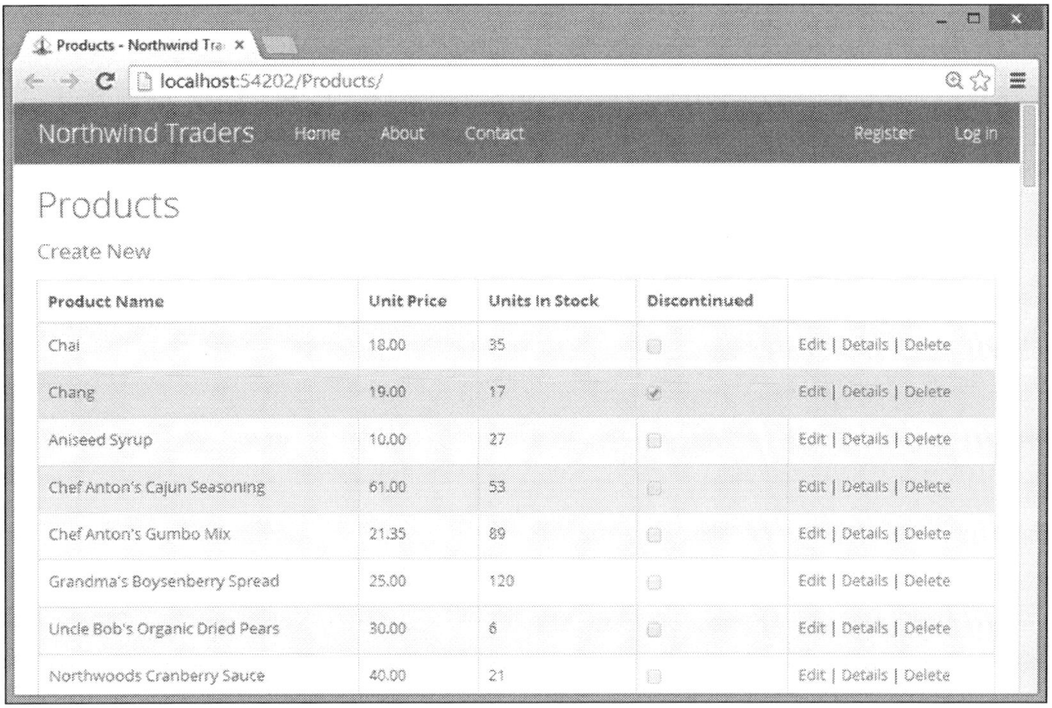

Bootstrap buttons

Bootstrap provides a wide range of buttons that comes in a variety of colors and sizes. The core buttons offer a choice of five colors and four sizes. The color and size of a button is applied using its `class` attribute. The list of classes to set the size of the button is as follows:

- `btn btn-default btn-xs`
- `btn btn-default btn-sm`
- `btn btn-default`
- `btn btn-default btn-lg`

To create four white/default buttons ranging from extra small to large, you'll implement the following HTML markup:

```
<div class="row">
    <!-- Standard button -->
    <button type="button" class="btn btn-default btn-xs">Default Extra
    Small</button>
    <button type="button" class="btn btn-default btn-sm">Default
    Small</button>
    <button type="button" class="btn btn-default">Default</button>
    <button type="button" class="btn btn-default btn-lg">Default
    Large</button>
</div>
```

Button colors are also specified by a class name. The following is a list of available color class names:

- `btn-default`
- `btn-primary`
- `btn-success`
- `btn-info`
- `btn-warning`

The range of buttons is illustrated in the following screenshot:

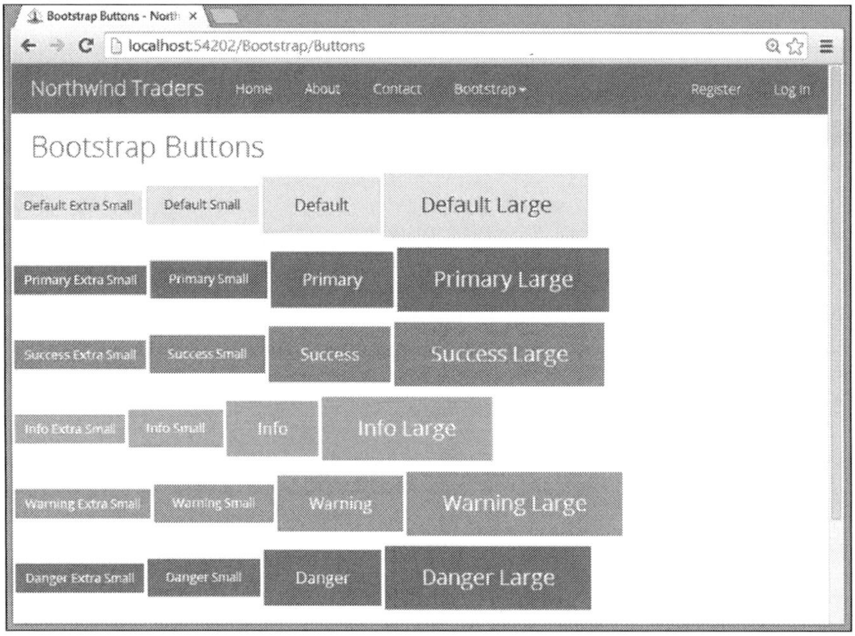

> In the previous screenshot, the buttons' edges are square, not rounded as the default Bootstrap bundles. This is because the example site is using a custom Bootstrap style. You can download a number of different Bootstrap styles from http://bootswatch.com/.

Form layout and elements

Forms make up a large section of most line-of-business applications; and therefore, applying a uniform style to all forms in your web application is not only visually pleasing but also provides your users with a friendlier interface. Bootstrap provides a range of CSS styles to enable you to create visually appealing forms.

Horizontal forms

The default create and edit templates for ASP.NET MVC scaffolding generate horizontal-styled Bootstrap forms. This is accomplished by automatically adding the form-horizontal class name to the <form> element. In the following code example, a horizontal login form is created using the Html.BeginForm helper method; this form contains two textboxes and a submit button:

```
@using (Html.BeginForm("Login", "Account", FormMethod.Post, new {
@class = "form-horizontal", role = "form" }))
{
    <div class="form-group">
        @Html.LabelFor(m => m.UserName, new { @class = "col-md-2
        control-label" })
        <div class="col-md-10">
            @Html.TextBoxFor(m => m.UserName, new { @class = "form-
        control" })
            @Html.ValidationMessageFor(m => m.UserName)
        </div>
    </div>
    <div class="form-group">
        @Html.LabelFor(m => m.Password, new { @class = "col-md-2
        control-label" })
        <div class="col-md-10">
            @Html.PasswordFor(m => m.Password, new { @class = "form-
            control" })
            @Html.ValidationMessageFor(m => m.Password)
        </div>
    </div>
```

```
        <div class="form-group">
            <div class="col-md-offset-2 col-md-10">
                <input type="submit" value="Log in" class="btn btn-
                default" />
            </div>
        </div>
    }
```

> Note that you can specify the width of the `form` elements by using the Bootstrap grid `col-*` class names.

It is also important to note that both the `Html.LabelFor` and `Html.TextBoxFor` helper methods are contained inside a `<div>` element with a class name of `form-group`. This is important to know when applying the Bootstrap validation styles to a `form` element. The resulting form will look similar to the following screenshot:

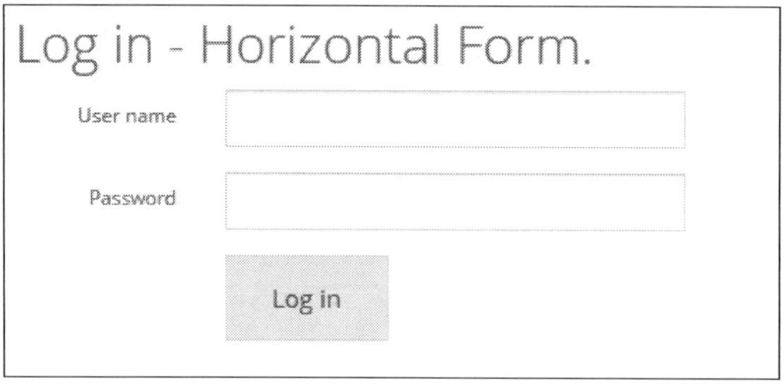

Vertical/Basic forms

The basic form in Bootstrap always displays its content in a vertical manner. For example, in the following code, we've taken the same login form we used previously and removed the `form-horizontal` class name from the `Html.BeginForm` helper:

```
    @using (Html.BeginForm("Login", "Account", FormMethod.Post, new { role
    = "form" }))
    {
        <div class="form-group">
            @Html.LabelFor(m => m.UserName)
            @Html.TextBoxFor(m => m.UserName, new { @class = "form-
            control" })
            @Html.ValidationMessageFor(m => m.UserName)
        </div>
```

```
        <div class="form-group">
            @Html.LabelFor(m => m.Password)
            @Html.PasswordFor(m => m.Password, new { @class = "form-
            control" })
            @Html.ValidationMessageFor(m => m.Password)
        </div>
        <div class="form-group">
            <input type="submit" value="Log in" class="btn btn-default" />
        </div>
    }
```

The result will look like the following screenshot in your browser:

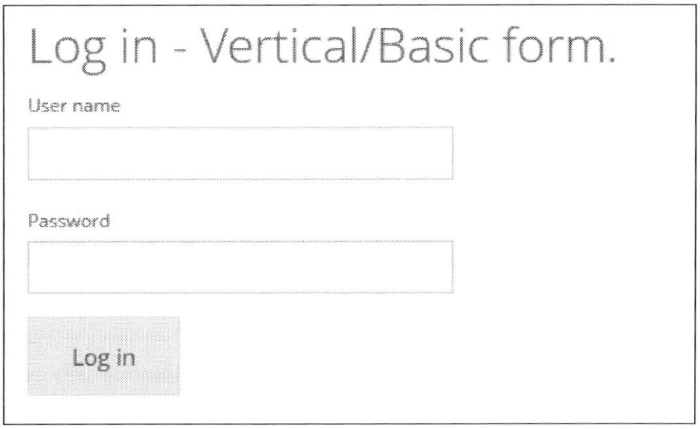

Inline forms

Inline forms are forms whose elements are aligned next to each other. Inline forms will only work on devices with viewports that have a width higher or equal to 768 px. It is a good practice to always include labels for your form elements in order for screen readers to be able to read your forms.

If you wish to hide the labels for your form elements, set its `label` class to `sr-only`. In the following code, we'll use the login form and set its `<form>` element's class to `form-inline`. Also, note the labels are not visible because of their `sr-only` class names:

```
@using (Html.BeginForm("Login", "Account", FormMethod.Post, new { @
class = "form-inline", role = "form" }))
{
    <div class="form-group">
```

```
            @Html.LabelFor(m => m.UserName, new { @class = "sr-only" })
            @Html.TextBoxFor(m => m.UserName, new { @class = "form-
            control", placeholder = "Enter your username" })
            @Html.ValidationMessageFor(m => m.UserName)
        </div>
        <div class="form-group">
            @Html.LabelFor(m => m.Password, new { @class = "sr-only" })
            @Html.PasswordFor(m => m.Password, new { @class = "form-
            control", placeholder = "Enter your username" })
            @Html.ValidationMessageFor(m => m.Password)
        </div>
        <div class="form-group">
            <input type="submit" value="Log in" class="btn btn-default" />
        </div>
    }
```

This will render the following form in your browser:

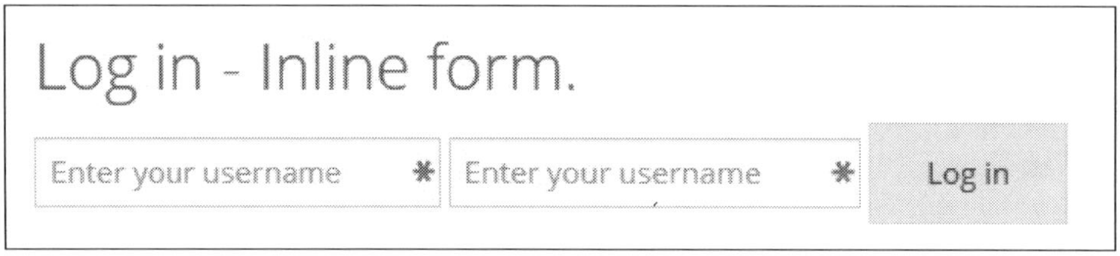

Bootstrap validation styles

The default ASP.NET MVC project template supports unobtrusive validation and automatically adds the required JavaScript libraries to your project. However, you'll notice that the default validation does not use the Bootstrap-specific CSS styles. When an input element fails validation, the jQuery validation plugin changes its class name to `input-validation-error`. This class name is declared inside the `Site.css` file and simply draws a red border around the invalid input element as displayed in the following screenshot:

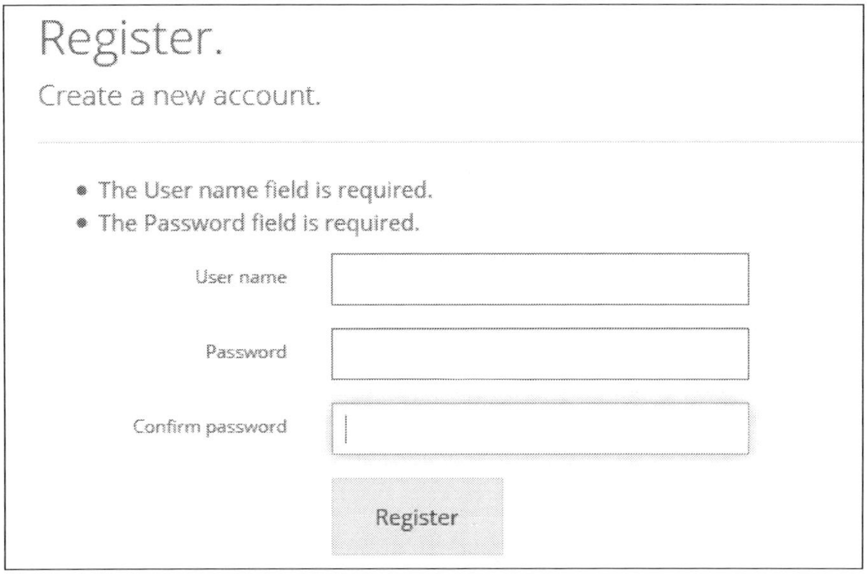

Bootstrap's validation styles, however, set the invalid input element's associated label's `font weight` to `bold` and draw a red border around the element. The reason the jQuery validation plugin does not work with the Bootstrap validation styles is because Bootstrap does not apply the validation style to the input element but adds the `has-error` class name to the parent element:

```
<div class="form-group has-error">
  <label class="control-label". for="name">Name</label>
  <input type="text" class="form-control" id="name">
</div>
```

In this code, the parent `<div>` element's class is changed to `form-group has-error`.

In order for our form to work with the Bootstrap validation classes without having to change the jQuery validation plugin directly, we first need to add a new JavaScript file called `jquery.validate.bootstrap.js` to our `Scripts` folder.

The following code will modify the default settings for the jQuery validation plugin by calling the `setDefaults` function. We then specify how the invalid element should be highlighted using the `highlight` function. In this function, we tell the validation plugin that it should find the closest element with a `.form-group` class and add the `has-error` class to it. In the `unhighlight` function, we remove the `has-error` class as follows:

```
$.validator.setDefaults({
  highlight: function (element) {
    $(element).closest('.form-group').addClass('has-error');
  },
  unhighlight: function (element) {
    $(element).closest('.form-group').removeClass('has-error');
  },
});
```

> You can read more about the jQuery validation plugin and its various settings on its project site located at `http://jqueryvalidation.org`.

Next, we need to add the new JavaScript file to the `jqueryval` bundle, which is specified in the `BundleConfig.cs` file. The current `jqueryval` bundle uses a wildcard to add all files that starts with `jquery.validate` to it. We need to change this to specify each file explicitly, as the bundling order is alphabetical for wildcard bundling and the `jquery.validation.bootstrap.js` file should be loaded after the jQuery validation library. The following code will add all the required validation libraries and files to our bundle:

```
bundles.Add(new ScriptBundle("~/bundles/jqueryval").Include(
            "~/Scripts/jquery.validate.js",
            "~/Scripts/jquery.validate.unobtrusive.js",
            "~/Scripts/jquery.validate.bootstrap.js"));
```

When building and running the project, you should now see the Bootstrap validation styles applied to invalid form elements as illustrated in the following screenshot:

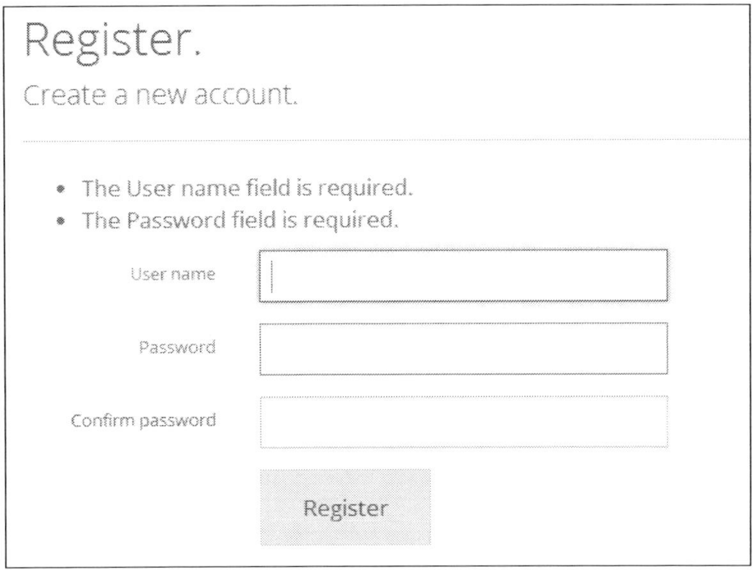

Creating editor templates for primitive types

Editor templates are used to automatically generate form input elements based on the datatype of an object's properties. ASP.NET MVC contains a number of standard editor templates but developers are also able to create their own. Editor templates are similar to partial views, but where partial views are rendered by name, editor templates are rendered by type.

When using Visual Studio's default scaffolding functionality to create an edit view for your model, it generates text input elements using the `EditorFor` HTML helper as follows:

```
@Html.EditorFor(model => model.CategoryName)
```

The EditorFor helper renders HTML for the model property based on its datatype. In the case of a string value, the resulting markup will look similar to the following:

```
<input type="text" name="CategoryName"
  id="CategoryName" data-val-required="The Category Name
    field is required."
      data-val="true" class="text-box single-line">
```

In this generated markup, the input element has a class of text-box single-line. For the text element to render correctly using the Bootstrap styles, the input element's class should be set to form-control.

In order for the EditorFor helper to generate the input element with the correct class, we need to create an editor template by completing the following steps:

1. First, create a new folder called EditorTemplates inside the Shared folder.
2. Next, add a new file called string.cshtml to the EditorTemplates folder and add the following code to it:

   ```
   @model string
   @Html.TextBox("", ViewData.TemplateInfo.FormattedModelValue, new {
   @class = "form-control"})
   ```

   In the preceding code, we created a textbox and passed in an empty string as the name for the textbox. This will cause ASP.NET MVC to use the model's property name as the name for the textbox. The value to show inside the textbox is specified by using the FormattedModelValue property of TemplateInfo. Lastly, we specify the HTML attributes for the element; in this case, we set its class property to form-control.

   Now, when a textbox is rendered using the EditorFor helper, the resulting HTML markup will look as follows:

   ```
   <input type="text" name="CategoryName" id="CategoryName" data-val-
   required="The Category Name field is required." data-val="true"
   class="form-control">
   ```

Creating editor templates for nonprimitive types

ASP.NET MVC enables developers to create editor templates for custom datatypes. For example, in the following screenshot, we have a form with a textbox and a multiline textbox:

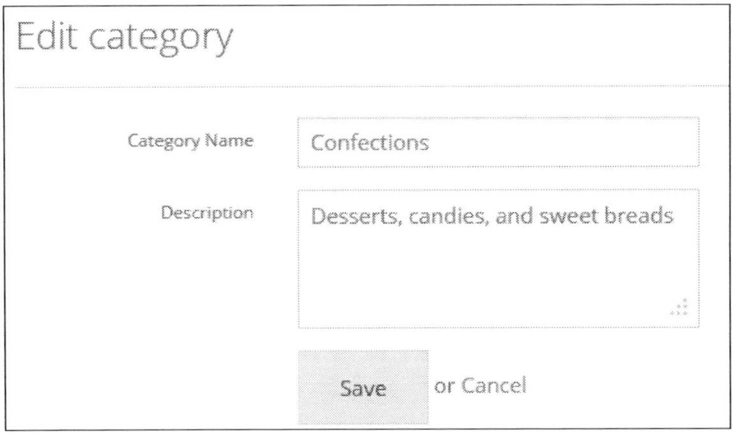

To generate multiline textboxes that look similar across our site and for example, always renders three rows, perform the following steps:

1. Add a new file called `MultilineText.cshtml` to the `EditorTemplates` folder.
2. Add the following code to the file:

```
@model string
@Html.TextArea("", ViewData.TemplateInfo.FormattedModelValue.
ToString(),new { @class = "form-control", rows = 3 })
```

   This code renders a text area element using the `TextArea` HTML helper and sets its `class` property to use the Bootstrap `form-control` style as well as specifying the number of rows the multiline textbox should render.

   In order for the view to use the correct editor template, we need to make an adjustment to our model. By adding a `DataType` attribute to the multiline property in our model, we can specify which editor template should be used when rendering the specific property. For example, in the following code, we'll specify that the `Description` property should use the `MultiLineText` editor template:

```
[DataType(DataType.MultilineText)]
public string Description { get; set; }
```

Bootstrap image classes

Images can be made responsive by setting their `class` attribute to `img-responsive`. This will scale the image in relation to its parent element by setting its `maximum width` to `100%` and `height` to `auto`.

You also have the option to shape images with either rounded corners, circles, or with an outer border. This is accomplished by setting the `<img>` element's class to one of the following Bootstrap classes:

- `img-rounded`
- `img-circle`
- `img-thumbnail`

In the following screenshot, we've displayed a list of employees and their pictures. The list of employees is retrieved from a database and passed to the view:

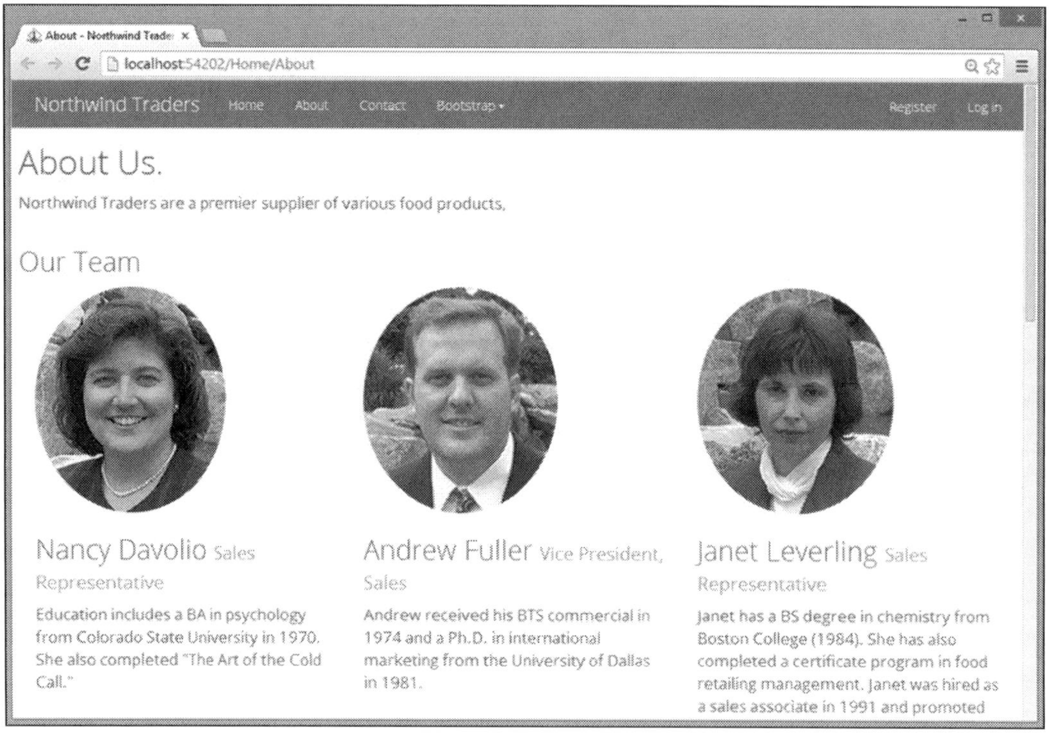

The code that achieves the preceding result (and can be viewed in the accompanying sample project) is as follows:

```
@model Northwind.Web.Models.EmployeeViewModel[]
<div class="container">
    <div class="row">
        <h2>About Us.</h2>
        <p>Northwind Traders are a premier supplier of various food
        products,</p>
    </div>
    <div class="row">
        <h3>Our Team</h3>
        @foreach (var item in Model)
        {
            <div class="col-md-4">
                <img src="@Url.Content("~/Images/employees/" + item.
                EmployeeID + ".png")" alt="@item.FirstName @item.
                LastName" class="img-circle img-responsive">
                <h3>
                    @item.FirstName @item.LastName <small>@item.
                    Title</small>
                </h3>
                <p>@item.Notes</p>
            </div>
        }
    </div>
</div>
```

In this code, we looped through each `employee` item in the model and rendered an `<img>` element using the `EmployeeID` property as the filename. Each `<img>` element's class attribute is set to `img-circle`, which will draw the image as a circle.

Summary

In this chapter, we've explored how to lay out various elements using the Bootstrap grid and form classes. We've also solved the problem of using the standard Bootstrap validation classes instead of the jQuery validation classes for form validation as well as streamlining the creation of form elements using ASP.NET's editor templates.

In the next chapter, we'll explore the various Bootstrap components including the Bootstrap navigation bar, input groups, progress bars, and alerts and how to implement them in your ASP.NET MVC project.

3

Using Bootstrap Components

Bootstrap provides over a dozen components to offer input groups, dropdowns, navigation, alerts, as well as iconography. Using these components in your web application, you can provide a consistent and easy-to-use interface for your users.

Bootstrap components are essentially made up by combining various existing Bootstrap elements, adding a number of unique class names, and representing a number of the common metaphors used on many websites.

In this chapter, we will cover the following topics:

- Using the Bootstrap navigation bar
- Implementing a context-sensitive search bar
- Using list groups, badges, and the media object
- Implementing page headers and breadcrumbs
- Creating a paged list using the `PagedList` library
- How to use alerts, input groups, and button dropdowns
- Implementing a progress bar that reports real-time progress with SignalR

The Bootstrap navigation bar

The Bootstrap navigation bar is one of the components that is used on a majority of sites using the Bootstrap framework. When creating an ASP.NET MVC website in Visual Studio, the default template generates all the HTML markup necessary for a standard navigation bar. The Bootstrap navigation bar looks like the following screenshot:

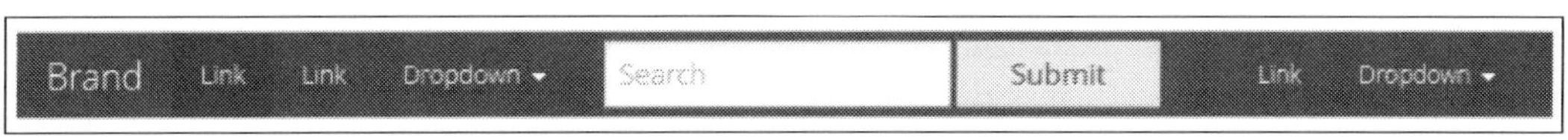

The following code inside the `_Layout.cshtml` file creates a `fixed-top` navigation bar, which is also responsive. When the site is opened on a device with a smaller screen size, it will display a button with three bars, and when you click on it, it will show the menu vertically:

```
<div class="navbar navbar-inverse navbar-fixed-top">
    <div class="container">
        <div class="navbar-header">
            <button type="button" class="navbar-toggle" data-
            toggle="collapse" data-target=".navbar-collapse">
                <span class="icon-bar"></span>
                <span class="icon-bar"></span>
                <span class="icon-bar"></span>
            </button>
            @Html.ActionLink("Northwind Traders", "Index", "Home",
            null, new { @class = "navbar-brand" })
        </div>
        <div class="navbar-collapse collapse">
            @Html.Partial("_BackendMenuPartial")
            @Html.Partial("_LoginPartial")
        </div>
    </div>
</div>
```

Note that we are using two partial views to generate the rest of the navigation bar based on whether the current user is logged in or not. We'll add a global `search` functionality to the navigation bar when the user is logged in; this will return results based on the page the user is currently visiting.

First, add the following code to the `_BackendMenuPartial` view; this will generate a search box inside the navigation bar:

```
@using (Html.BeginForm("Index", "Search", FormMethod.Post, new {@class
= "navbar-form navbar-left", role = "search"}))
{
    <div class="form-group">
        @Html.TextBox("searchquery","",new { @id="searchquery",
        @class="form-control input-sm", placeholder="Search" })
        @Html.Hidden("fromcontroller", @ViewContext.RouteData.
        Values["controller"], new  { @id = "fromcontroller" })
    </div>
    <button type="submit" class="btn btn-default btn-xs">GO</button>
}
```

You'll notice that in the preceding code, we have a hidden field called `fromcontroller` that contains the name of the current controller. We get this from the `RouteData` object, which is a property on `ViewContext`. This information will be used to return search results based on the current page.

The form will perform an HTTP `POST` method to the `Index` action of the `Search` controller; this in turn will check the controller name from which the request came and return the appropriate data and view. The code that performs the search is as follows:

```
[HttpPost]
public ActionResult Index(string searchquery, string fromcontroller)
{
    switch (fromcontroller)
    {
        case "Products":
            return RedirectToAction("SearchProductsResult", new {
            query = searchquery });

        case "Customers":
            return RedirectToAction("SearchCustomersResult", new {
            query = searchquery });

        case "Employees":
            return RedirectToAction("SearchEmployeesResult", new {
            query = searchquery });
    }
    return View();
}

public ActionResult SearchCustomersResult(string query)
{
    ViewBag.SearchQuery = query;
    var results = _context.Customers.Where(p => p.CompanyName.
    Contains(query)
        || p.ContactName.Contains(query)
        || p.City.Contains(query)
        || p.Country.Contains(query)).ToList();
    return View(results);
}
```

List groups

List groups are flexible components that either display simple lists of elements or can be combined with other elements to create complex lists with custom content. Our search will redirect us to the `SearchProductsResult` view when the user searches for products. This view uses a list group to display the product items found. The method that retrieves the products from the database is as follows:

```
public ActionResult SearchProductsResult(string query)
{
    ViewBag.SearchQuery = query;
    var results = _context.Products.Where(p => p.ProductName.
    Contains(query)).ToList();
    return View(results);
}
```

The Razor markup for the view represents the following:

```
@model IEnumerable<Northwind.Data.Models.Product>
@{
    ViewBag.Title = "Product Search Results";
    Layout = "~/Views/Shared/_Layout.cshtml";
}
<div class="container">
    <div class="page-header">
        <h1>Product Results <small>Results for your search term:
        "@ViewBag.SearchQuery"</small></h1>
    </div>
    <ul class="list-group">
        @foreach (var item in Model)
        {
            <a href="@Url.Action("Edit","Products", new { id=@
            item.ProductID})" class="list-group-item">@item.
            ProductName <span class="badge">@item.UnitsInStock</
            span></a>
        }
    </ul>
</div>
```

In this markup, the product items are loaded into an unordered list element `<ul>` as anchor `<a>` elements. Each anchor element's class name should be set to `list-group-item`. The view should look like the following screenshot in your browser:

Badges

Badges are used to highlight items. You would normally see badges to indicate the number of new or unread items, depending on the type of application. We used the following badges on the product's search result page to indicate the number of units currently in stock:

```
<a href="@Url.Action("Edit","Products", new { id=@item.ProductID})"
class="list-group-item">@item.ProductName <span class="badge">@item.
UnitsInStock</span></a>
```

Adding a badge to an element is as simple as adding a `<span>` element and setting its class name to `badge`.

The media object

The media object component can be used to build hierarchal style lists such as blog comments or tweets. In our example application, we used the media object to return a search result view when the user searches for employees. As the `Northwind` database contains a field (`ReportsTo`) that indicates which employee the other employees report to, the media object component would be ideal to indicate this visually. The method that searches for the employees and returns the results to the view is as follows:

```
public ActionResult SearchEmployeesResult(string query)
{
    ViewBag.SearchQuery = query;
    var results = _context.Employees.Where(p => p.FirstName.
    Contains(query)
        || p.LastName.Contains(query)
        || p.Notes.Contains(query)).ToList();
    return View(results);
}
```

The view for the employee's search result uses the media object component to style the employee information and display the employee's photos as follows:

```
@model IEnumerable<Northwind.Data.Models.Employee>
@{
    ViewBag.Title = "Employees Search Results";
    Layout = "~/Views/Shared/_Layout.cshtml";
}
<div class="container">
    <div class="page-header">
        <h1>Employees Results <small>Results for your search term:
        "@ViewBag.SearchQuery"</small></h1>
    </div>
    @foreach (var item in Model)
    {
        <div class="media">
            <a class="pull-left" href="@Url.Action("Edit",
            "Employees", new { id = @item.EmployeeID })">
                <img class="media-object" src="@Url.Content("~/
                Images/employees/" + @item.EmployeeID + ".png")"
                alt="@item.FirstName" width="64" height="64">
            </a>
            <div class="media-body">
                <h4 class="media-heading">@item.FirstName @item.
                LastName</h4>
                @item.Notes
                @foreach (var emp in @item.ReportingEmployees)
                {
                    <div class="media">
                        <a href="#" class="pull-left">
                            <img alt="@emp.FirstName" src="@
Url.Content("~/Images/employees/" + @emp.EmployeeID + ".png")"
class="media-object" width="64" height="64">
                        </a>
                        <div class="media-body">
                            <h4 class="media-heading">@emp.FirstName
                            @emp.LastName</h4>
                            @emp.Title
                        </div>
                    </div>
                }
            </div>
        </div>

    }
</div>
```

The media object component is built using a combination of elements with the class names of `media`, `media-heading` and `media-body`. The `media-object` class name is used to indicate media objects such as images, video, or audio. The resulting view should look similar to the following screenshot:

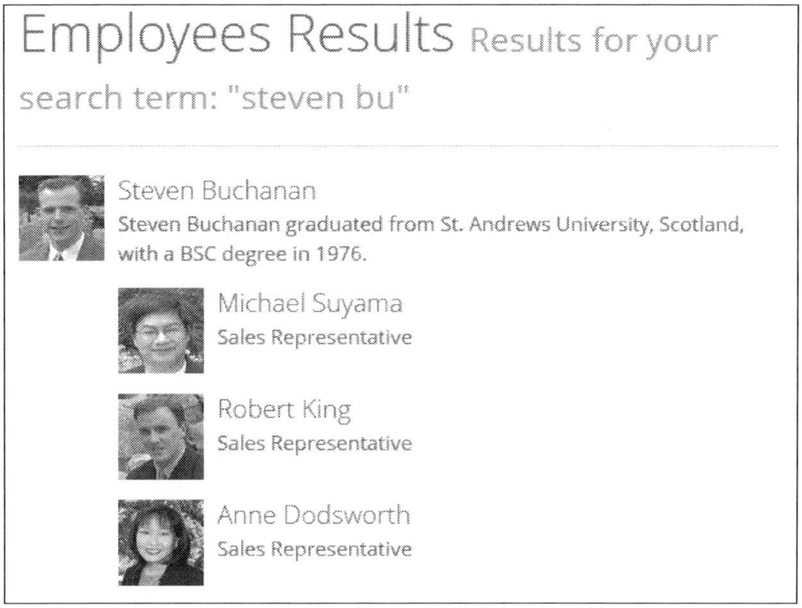

Page headers

The Bootstrap page header is used to provide a clear indication to the user that the page consists of a heading that introduces them to the page they are visiting. The page header is essentially a `<h1>` element wrapped inside a `<div>` element with a class name of `page-header`. You can also utilize the `<small>` element to provide additional information to the user about the page. Bootstrap also adds a horizontal line below the page header that provides a visual separation from the rest of the page.

The following HTML markup creates a page header:

```
<div class="page-header">
    <h1>Categories <small>Add, edit and delete product categories</
    small></h1>
</div>
```

This markup will generate the following screenshot in your browser:

Breadcrumb

Breadcrumb is a common metaphor used in web design to indicate to the user what their current location is inside a navigation tree. It is similar to a file path in Windows Explorer. Breadcrumb is ideal for a site with many subnavigation levels and allows the user to navigate between the varied parent and child pages.

In the following markup, we'll use a combination of Razor and HTML to build a `breadcrumb` component with which the user can navigate back to the home page or the `Manage` page:

```
<ol class="breadcrumb">
    <li>@Html.ActionLink("Home","Index","Home")</li>
    <li>@Html.ActionLink("Manage", "Index", "Manage")</li>
    <li class="active">Categories</li>
</ol>
```

The preceding markup contains an ordered list `<ol>` element with a class name of `breadcrumb`. Each child element of the breadcrumb is added as a list item `<li>` element. To indicate to the user that the last level of the breadcrumb is the active page, we set its `<li>` element's class name to `active`. The result of the previous code will look like the following screenshot when visiting the page:

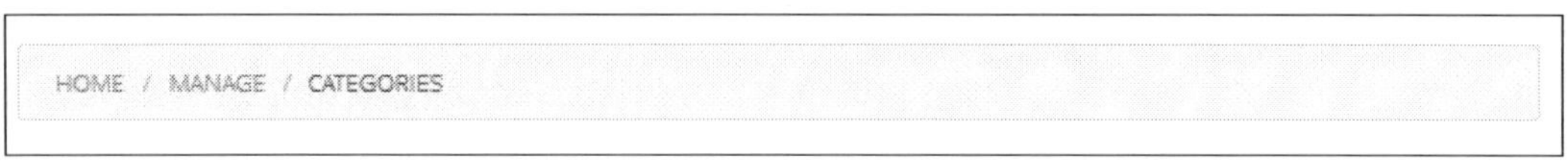

Pagination

Pagination is used to divide content, usually lists, into separate pages. For example, when scaffolding a list view, the default scaffolding template generates a table that contains a row for each item in the collection you pass into the view. This is fine for small amounts of data, but if the list contains hundreds of items, your page will take a very long time to load. Ideally, we would like to split our list view into a manageable view that has five items per page. In the following screenshot, we've changed the **Products** page's table to use pagination:

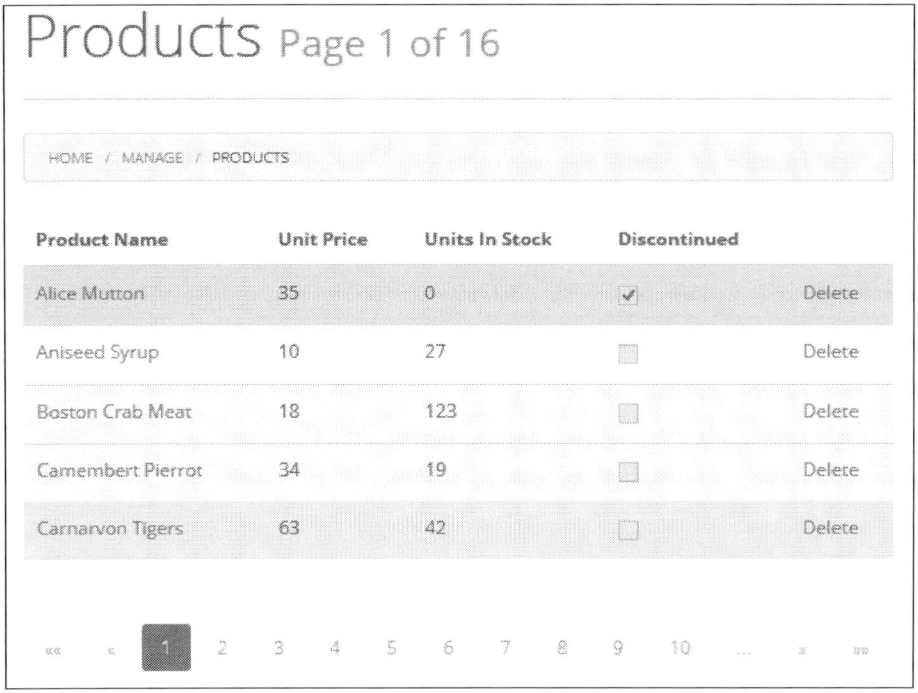

The aforementioned view is accomplished using the `PagedList.Mvc` NuGet package and completing the following steps:

1. To install it, run the following command inside the Visual Studio **Package Manager Console**:

   ```
   Install-Package PagedList.Mvc
   ```

2. This command will add the necessary dependencies to your project. Next, open your controller action and change its code to the following:

   ```
   public ActionResult Index(int? page)
   {
       var models = _context.Products.Project().
       To<ProductViewModel>().OrderBy(p => p.ProductName);
       int pageSize = 5;
       int pageNumber = (page ?? 1);
       return View(models.ToPagedList(pageNumber, pageSize));
   }
   ```

   In the preceding code, we changed the `action` method to accept an integer parameter called `page`. This parameter is used to indicate which page of the list the user is currently viewing. We then retrieved a list of products from our database and ordered it using the `ProductName` property.

The `pageSize` variable is used to set the number of items each page should display. We then returned the product items as `PagedList`. The `PagedList` object is part of the `PagedList.Mvc` library that we installed via NuGet earlier.

3. Next, open the associated view and add the following code to the top of the file:

```
@using PagedList.Mvc;
@model PagedList.IPagedList<Northwind.Web.Models.ProductViewModel>
```

4. The `using` statement tells the view to reference the `PagedList` library. We then set the view's model to a `PagedList` representation of our `ProductViewModel` object.
5. You do not need to change anything in your existing markup; however, to indicate the current page number, add the following code to your page:

```
Page @(Model.PageCount < Model.PageNumber ? 0 : Model.PageNumber)
of @Model.PageCount
```

6. The preceding code will display the current page number and the total number of pages. To add a paging element to the page that conforms to the default Bootstrap styling, add the following code just below the closing tag of the `<table>` element:

```
@Html.PagedListPager(Model, page => Url.Action("Index", new { page
}), PagedListRenderOptions.ClassicPlusFirstAndLast)
```

In the preceding code, we used the `PagedListPager` HTML helper that is included in the `PagedList` library to display a pagination element; this element contains all the page numbers as well as the buttons that will navigate to the first and last page. You'll notice that the last parameter of the `PagedListPager` helper supports nine different pagination layouts. They are as follows:

- `Classic`
- `ClassicPlusFirstAndLast`
- `Minimal`
- `MinimalWithItemCountText`
- `MinimalWithPageCountText`
- `OnlyShowFivePagesAtATime`
- `PageNumbersOnly`
- `TwitterBootstrapPager`
- `TwitterBootstrapPagerAligned`

Setting the parameter to `PagedListRenderOptions.TwitterBootstrapPagerAligned` will show two buttons, titled **Older** and **Newer**. They are aligned to the edges of the container, as shown in the following screenshot:

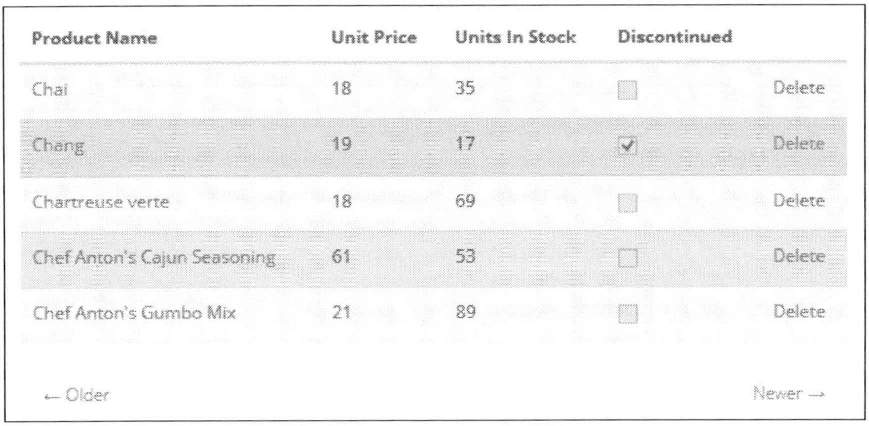

Setting the parameter to `PagedListRenderOptions.TwitterBootstrapPager` will add the **Previous** and **Next** buttons that are centered below `<table>`:

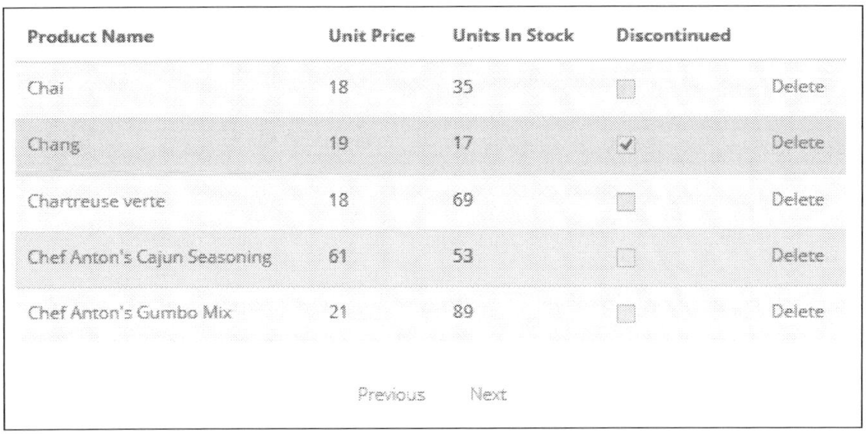

The `PagedList` library supports the default Bootstrap styles out of the box; this means that you do not need to do anything specific to enable the correct styling.

Input groups

Input groups are another way to provide the user with additional information about the data you expect them to enter in a specific form element. Bootstrap provides classes to add sections either before or after an input element. These sections can contain either text or any of the 200 Glyphicons included in Bootstrap.

> Bootstrap comes prepackaged with 200 Glyphicon Halfling icons. Normally, the Glyphicon Halflings icons that are set are not free, but their creator made them available to Bootstrap free of charge. You can read more about them at `http://getbootstrap.com/components/`.

To create a text input element to indicate to the user that we require them to enter a phone number into the field, we'll use the following markup:

```
<div class="form-group">
    @Html.LabelFor(model => model.Phone, new { @class = "control-label
    col-md-2" })
    <div class="col-sm-4 input-group">
        <span class="input-group-addon">
            <span class="glyphicon glyphicon-phone-alt"></span>
        </span>
        @Html.EditorFor(model => model.Phone)
        @Html.ValidationMessageFor(model => model.Phone)
    </div>
</div>
```

The result of this markup will be a text input element with a gray section to its left, with an image of a telephone inside it, as illustrated in the following screenshot:

We can also create input groups that are aligned on the right-hand side of text inputs and that contain text instead of images. For example, the following markup creates a text input field that indicates to the user that we only require the first part of an e-mail address and that the last part will automatically be appended:

```
<div class="form-group">
    @Html.LabelFor(model => model.Email, new { @class = "control-label
    col-md-2" })
    <div class="col-sm-4 input-group">
        @Html.EditorFor(model => model.Email)
        <span class="input-group-addon">@@northwind.com</span>
    </div>
</div>
```

The result of the preceding markup will look like the following screenshot in your browser:

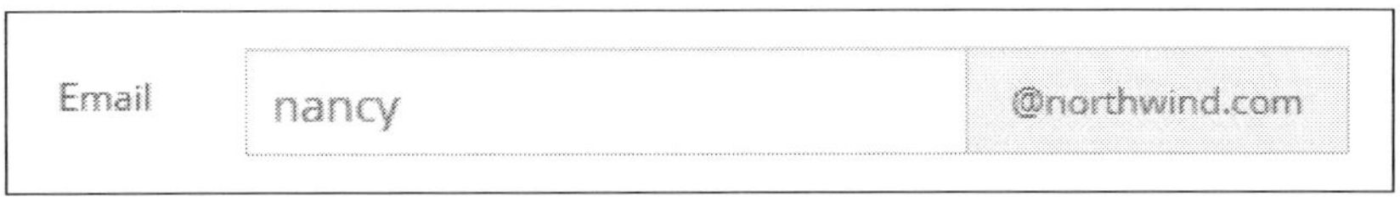

You can also create a text input with a gray section on both sides with the following code:

```
<div class="form-group">
    @Html.LabelFor(model => model.UnitPrice, new { @class = "col-sm-2
    control-label" })
    <div class="col-sm-2 input-group">
        <span class="input-group-addon">$</span>
        @Html.TextBoxFor(model => model.UnitPrice, new { @class =
        "form-control" })
        <span class="input-group-addon">.00</span>
        @Html.ValidationMessageFor(model => model.UnitPrice)
    </div>
</div>
```

In the preceding code, we created a text input with a gray section with a dollar sign on the left-hand side and a gray section that contains `.00` on the right-hand side. This will indicate to the user that we expect a round number and that the system always expects zero decimals, as shown in the following screenshot:

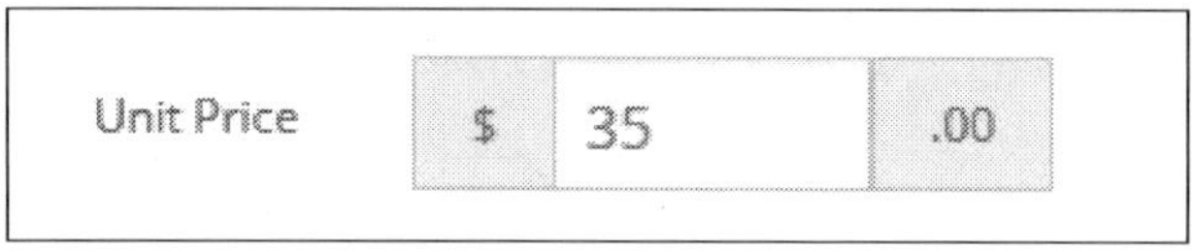

Button dropdowns

Button dropdowns are useful when you need a button that can perform multiple related actions. For example, you could have a save button that saves a record, but you would also like to give the user an option to save the record and automatically show a new empty form to create another record. This will be beneficial to the user when they need to create multiple records of the same type.

For example, the following code creates a button dropdown inside a form that will create a `save` button with two additional actions:

```
<div class="form-group">
    <div class="col-sm-offset-2 col-sm-10">
        <div class="btn-group">
            <button type="submit" class="btn btn-primary
            btn-sm">Save</button>
            <button type="button" class="btn btn-primary btn-sm
            dropdown-toggle" data-toggle="dropdown">
                <span class="caret"></span>
                <span class="sr-only">Toggle Dropdown</span>
            </button>
            <ul class="dropdown-menu" role="menu">
                <li><a href="#" id="savenew">Save & New</a></li>
                <li class="divider"></li>
                <li><a href="#" id="duplicate">Duplicate</a></li>
            </ul>
        </div>
    </div>
</div>
```

The result will look like the following screenshot in your browser:

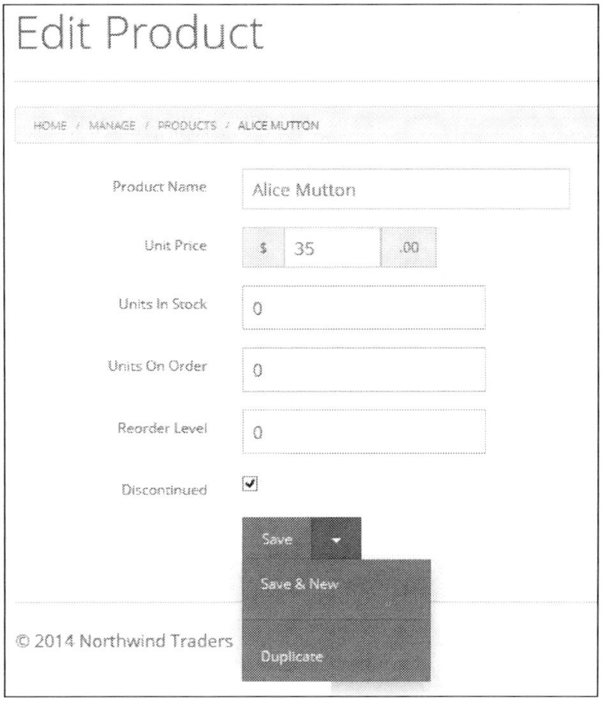

Alerts

The alert component is used to provide visual feedback to the user. This can be used to provide the user with either confirmation messages that a record has been saved, warning messages that an error occurred, or an information message based on a system event.

Bootstrap provides four differently styled alerts. For instance, the following markup generates a green, blue, orange, and red alert box:

```
<div class="alert alert-success"><strong>Success. You have
successfully saved the file.</strong></div>
<div class="alert alert-info"><strong>Info. Something has just
happened.</strong></div>
<div class="alert alert-warning"><strong>Warning! The file size is too
big.</strong></div>
<div class="alert alert-danger"><strong>Danger! The file could not be
saved.</strong></div>
```

The alert boxes should look similar to the following screenshot in your browser:

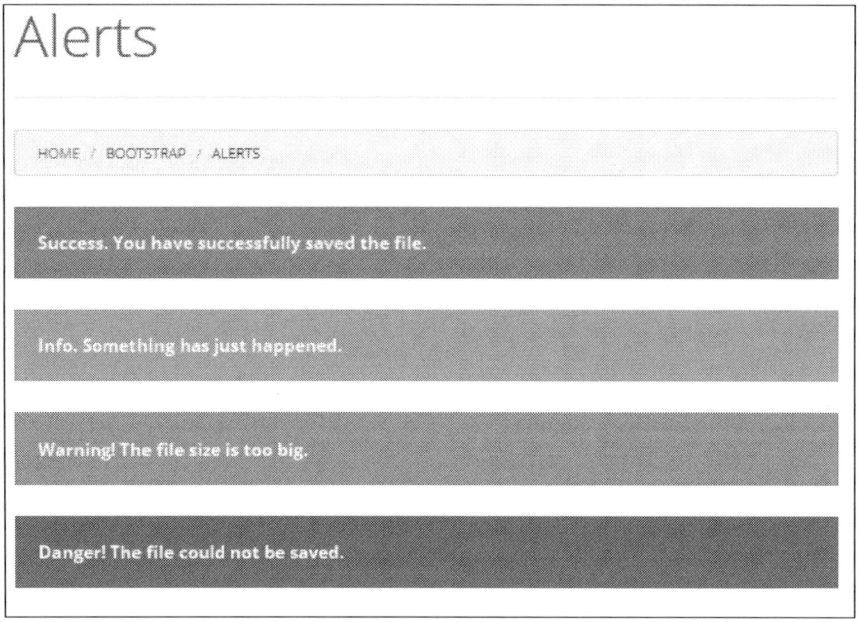

A dismissible alert is an alert that can be closed by the user by clicking on a small **X** icon in its top right-hand corner. In order to create a dismissible alert, you can use the `alert-dismissible` class name as follows:

```
<div class="alert alert-warning alert-Dismissible" role="alert">
    <button type="button" class="close" data-dismiss="alert"><span
aria-hidden="true">&times;</span><span class="sr-only">Close</span></
button>
    <strong>Alert!</strong> This is a dismissible alert.
</div>
```

> You can refer to this book's accompanying sample project for an indication of how to display specifically styled alerts directly from your ASP.NET MVC controllers. These alerts are adapted from Matt Honeycutt's example on GitHub: `https://github.com/MattHoneycutt/Fail-Tracker`.

Progress bars

Progress bars are a metaphor used with traditional desktop as well as web development to provide visual feedback to a user on the progress of a task or action. Bootstrap provides a number of differently styled progress bars.

The basic progress bar

The basic Bootstrap progress bar displays a plain blue-colored progress bar. Adding a `<span>` element with a class name of `sr-only` is good practice in order to allow screen readers to read the progress percentage. The following markup generates a basic progress bar with a heading:

```
<h4>Basic Progressbar</h4>
<div class="progress">
    <div class="progress-bar" role="progressbar" aria-valuenow="80"
    aria-valuemin="0" aria-valuemax="100" style="width: 80%;">
        <span class="sr-only">80% Complete</span>
    </div>
</div>
```

The result of this markup is shown in the following screenshot:

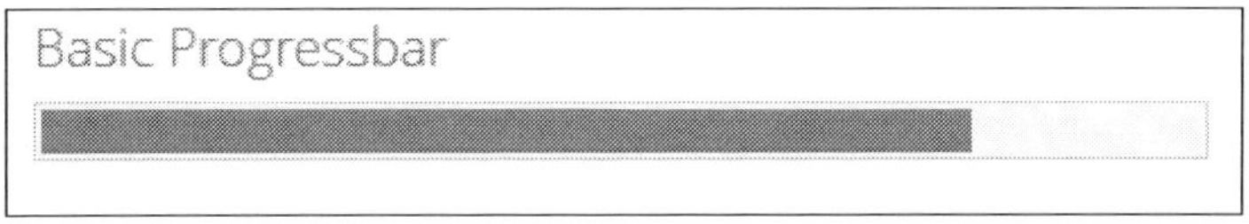

You can also display an inline label for the progress bar by adding text inside its `<div>` element:

```
<h4>Basic Progressbar with label</h4>
<div class="progress">
    <div id="progressbarTitle" class="progress-bar" role="progressbar"
    aria-valuenow="60" aria-valuemin="0" aria-valuemax="100"
    style="width: 60%;">
        60%
    </div>
</div>
```

The result of this code is shown in the following screenshot:

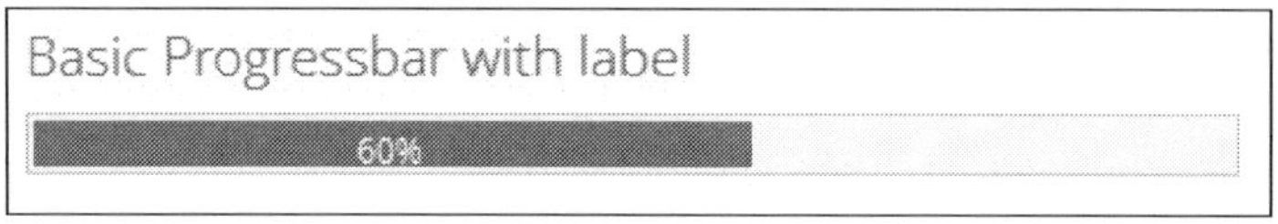

Contextual progress bars

You can use the same button and alert style classes to generate differently colored progress bars. This is accomplished by setting the progress bar's class name to one of the following:

- `progress-bar-success`
- `progress-bar-info`
- `progress-bar-warning`
- `progress-bar-danger`

The result is illustrated in the following screenshot:

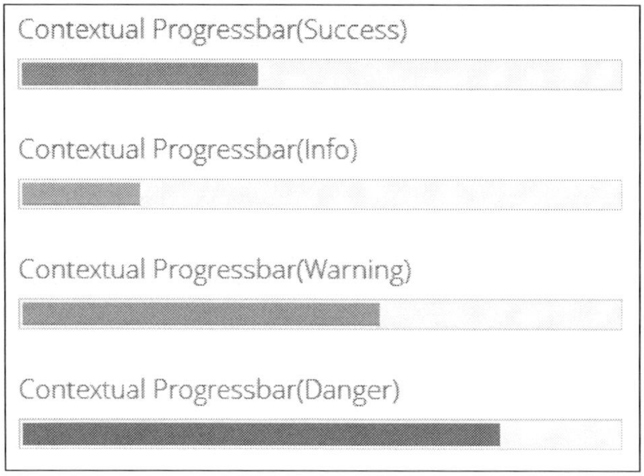

Striped and animated progress bars

To generate progress bars with a gradient striped effect, add the class name of `progress-striped` to the progress bar's parent `<div>` element:

```
<h4>Striped Progressbar(Danger)</h4>
<div class="progress progress-striped">
    <div class="progress-bar progress-bar-danger"
    role="progressbar" aria-valuenow="80" aria-valuemin="0"
    aria-valuemax="100" style="width: 80%">
        <span class="sr-only">80% Complete (danger)</span>
    </div>
</div>
```

This result is shown in the following screenshot:

To add an animated effect that will give the impression that the stripes on the progress bar are moving, simply add a class of `active` to its parent `<div>` element:

```
<div class="progress progress-striped active">
    <div class="progress-bar progress-bar-danger" role="progressbar"
    aria-valuenow="80" aria-valuemin="0" aria-valuemax="100"
    style="width: 80%">
        <span class="sr-only">80% Complete (success)</span>
    </div>
</div>
```

Dynamically updating the progress bar's percentage

A progress bar is only worth using when it actually gives feedback on the progress of a specific task. To update the progress bar dynamically using ASP.NET MVC, perform the following steps:

1. Add the `SignalR` NuGet package to our project by running the following command in the Visual Studio **Package Manager Console**:

   ```
   Install-Package Microsoft.AspNet.SignalR
   ```

> `SignalR` is a library for ASP.NET; this library makes it very easy to add real-time functionality and feedback to your applications. You can read more about it at `www.signalr.net`.

2. Next, add a new folder called `Hubs` to your project, and add a new class called `ProgressbarHub.cs` to the folder. Change its code to the following code:

```
using System.Threading;
using Microsoft.AspNet.SignalR;

namespace Northwind.Web.Hubs
{
    public class ProgressbarHub : Hub
    {
        public void SendProgress()
        {
            for (int i = 0; i <= 100; i++)
            {
                Thread.Sleep(50);
                Clients.Caller.sendMessage(i + "%");
            }
        }
    }
}
```

3. In the preceding code, our class inherits from the SignalR `Hub` class and contains a single method called `SendProgress`, which will increment a variable and send the value to any SignalR clients using the `sendMessage` method.
4. Next, we add a reference to the SignalR virtual path. Open the `_Layout.cshtml` file, and add the following line to the bottom of the file:

```
<script src="~/signalr/hubs"></script>
```

5. We'll also add a reference to the SignalR JavaScript library in our existing bundles. Open the `BundleConfig.cs` file located in the `App_Start` folder, and change the `jquery` bundle to include the SignalR library as follows:

```
bundles.Add(new ScriptBundle("~/bundles/jquery").Include(
            "~/Scripts/jquery-{version}.js",
            "~/Scripts/jquery.signalR-2.0.3.js"));
```

6. Finally, on the page where we have our progress bars, add the following script inside the `Scripts` section:

```
@section scripts
{
    <script type="text/javascript" language="javascript">
        $("#start").click(function () {
            $(".progress-bar").width('0%');
            var progressNotifier = $.connection.progressbarHub;
            progressNotifier.client.sendMessage = function
            (message) {
                updateProgress(message);
            };

            $.connection.hub.start().done(function () {
                progressNotifier.server.sendProgress();
            });
        });

        function updateProgress(message) {
            $(".progress-bar").width(message);
            $("#progressbarTitle").html(message + ' Complete');
        }
    </script>
}
```

The preceding code will be executed when the user clicks on a button with an ID of `start`. It will first set all the progress bars on the page's width to `0` and initialize a connection to the server. We then set the function name that will be called from the server side. In this scenario, the JavaScript function's name is `updateProgress`.

Finally, we establish a connection to the server and start the server-side operation. As you can see, we invoked the `sendProgress` function—this is the name of the method declared inside the `ProgressbarHub` class.

As a result of the code, you will see that all the progress bars on the page will increase their values from 0 to 100.

Summary

In this chapter, we explored the many different Bootstrap components as well as learned how to use them in your ASP.NET MVC project. We also looked at NuGet packages to aid you in creating paged lists and to dynamically update progress bars.

In the next chapter, we'll delve deeper into the Bootstrap components by investigating how to add more interactivity to your site using the Bootstrap JavaScript plugins.

4
Using Bootstrap JavaScript Plugins

Bootstrap's JavaScript features are all built on top of the jQuery library and either provide completely new functionality or extend the functionality of the existing Bootstrap components.

The plugins can be used by simply adding data attributes to your page elements, but they also provide a rich programmatic API, if needed.

In this chapter, we will cover the following topics:

- How to use dropdowns and create a cascading dropdown
- How to use modal dialogs
- How to partition your views with tabs
- How to implement tooltips and popovers
- How to use the accordion component
- How to create a slideshow using the carousel

> In order to use Bootstrap plugins, we'll need to include the `bootstrap.js` or `bootstrap.min.js` file in our project. This file contains all the Bootstrap plugins, but if you do not intend to use every plugin in your project, it is a good idea to customize which components are to be included in the `bootstrap.js` file. This will make the size of the Bootstrap library smaller and allow the website to load faster. To access these plugins, navigate to `http://getbootstrap.com/customize/` and select the plugins that you'll be using in your project.

Data attributes versus the programmatic API

Bootstrap offers the ability to use its plugins entirely through the HTML markup. This means that in order to use most of the plugins, you do not need to write a single line of JavaScript. Using data attributes is the recommended approach and should be your first option when using Bootstrap plugins.

For example, to allow an `alert` element to be dismissible, you'll add the `data-dismiss="alert"` attribute to either a `button` or `anchor` element, as illustrated in the following code:

```
<div class="alert alert-danger">
    <button data-dismiss="alert" class="close" type="button">x</
    button>
    <strong>Warning</strong> Shuttle launch in t-minus 10 seconds.
</div>
```

You also have the option to perform the same action using the programmatic API via JavaScript. The following code uses jQuery to close a specific `alert` element when the user clicks on a button:

```
<button class="close" type="button" onclick="$('#myalert').
alert('close')">x</button>
```

Cascading dropdowns

You can add drop-down menus to almost any Bootstrap component using the dropdown plugin. A cascading dropdown is a dropdown that updates its data based on a value selected in another dropdown. To add cascading dropdowns, perform the following steps:

1. We'll add drop-down menus to two buttons which will list the region and territory data that was retrieved from a database. When the user selects a region, the **Territory** drop-down list will update to show only those territories associated with the selected region. The following screenshot illustrates the end result:

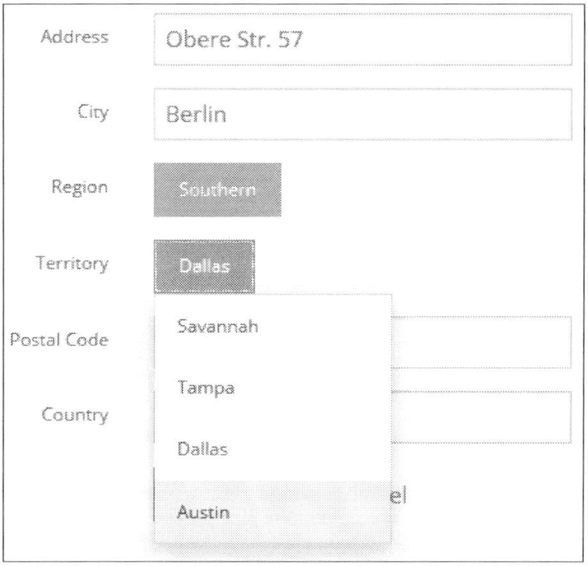

2. The two drop-down menus will be used in our **Edit Customer** view, and in order for the list of territories and regions to be accessible in our view, we'll first add them to the `ViewBag` object using the following code:

```
public ActionResult Edit(int id)
{
    var model = _context.Customers.First(c => c.CustomerId == id);
    ViewBag.RegionId = new SelectList(_context.Regions,
    "RegionId", "RegionDescription", model.RegionId);
    ViewBag.TerritoryId = new SelectList(_context.Territories.
    Where(t => t.RegionId == model.RegionId), "TerritoryId",
    "TerritoryDescription", model.TerritoryId);
    return View(model);
}
```

In this code, we first loaded the requested customer from the database and then added a list of regions and territories from the database to the `ViewBag` object. You will notice that we only retrieved the territories in the selected customer's region.

3. Next, we add the Razor markup to our view to create two buttons with drop-down menus. In the following code, we'll create two new Bootstrap form groups that contain a label for the `region` and `territory` properties as well as hidden elements that will carry the selected region and territory ID. We iterate over the regions and territories that were passed to the view via the `ViewBag` object and build up the menu items.

```
<div class="form-group">
    @Html.LabelFor(model => model.RegionId,
    new { @class = "control-label col-md-2" })
    @Html.HiddenFor(model => model.RegionId)
    <div class="col-md-10">
        <div id="regiondropdown" class="dropdown">
            <button id="regionbutton" class="btn btn-sm btn-info"
            data-toggle="dropdown">@Model.Region.
            RegionDescription</button>
            <ul class="dropdown-menu">
                @foreach (var item in ViewBag.RegionId)
                {
                    <li><a href="#" tabindex="-1" data-value="@
                    item.Value">@item.Text</a></li>
                }
            </ul>
        </div>
    </div>
</div>
<div class="form-group">
    @Html.LabelFor(model => model.TerritoryId, new { @class =
    "control-label col-md-2" })
    @Html.HiddenFor(model => model.TerritoryId)
    <div class="col-md-10">
        <div id="territorydropdown" class="dropdown">
            <button id="territorybutton" class="btn btn-
            sm btn-info" data-toggle="dropdown">@Model.Territory.
            TerritoryDescription</button>
            <ul id="territories" class="dropdown-menu">
                @foreach (var item in ViewBag.TerritoryId)
                {
                    <li><a href="#" tabindex="-1" data-value="@
                    item.Value">@item.Text</a></li>
                }
            </ul>
        </div>
    </div>
</div>
```

> Note that we're setting the `tabindex` item of the `anchor` element `<a>` inside the menu to `-1`. This is done to prevent the element from being part of the tab order.

4. Next, add a new partial view called `Territories.cshtml` to your project. We'll use this partial view to load the territories each time the user changes the region. In order to load the partial view, we'll need to add a new method to `CustomerController` that returns `PartialViewResult`. The code for this method is as follows:

```
public PartialViewResult Territories(int regionId)
{
    ViewBag.TerritoryId = new SelectList(_context.Territories.
    Where(t => t.RegionId == regionId), "TerritoryId",
    "TerritoryDescription");
    return PartialView();
}
```

   This method receives a region ID as a parameter and then loads the region's associated territories into the `ViewBag` object. Finally, the method returns the `Territories` partial view we've created earlier.

5. Finally, in order to load the associated territories when the user selects a different region, we'll need to add a bit of JavaScript to our page. To do this, create a new section in the view, and add the following JavaScript code to it:

```
@section scripts{
    <script type="text/javascript">
        $('#regiondropdown li a').click(function () {
            var $this = $(this);
            var region = $this.data('value');
            var regionName = $this.text();
            $('#RegionId').val(region);
            $.get("/Customers/Territories", { regionId: region })
            .done(function (data) {
                $('#regionbutton').text(regionName);
                $('#territorybutton').text('Select Territory');
                $('#territories').html(data);
            });
        });

        $('body').on("click", '#territories li a', function () {
            var $this = $(this);
            var territory = $this.data('value');
            var territoryName = $this.text();
```

```
                $('#TerritoryId').val(territory);
                $('#territorybutton').text(territoryName);
            });

        </script>
    }
```

The preceding JavaScript creates a click handler for the `region` drop-down element and saves the selected region ID to a variable. This variable is then passed to the jQuery `get` method, which in turn makes a request to the `Territories` method in `CustomerController`. The `Territories` method returns a partial view with a list of territories whose region IDs match the received parameter.

The code also uses the jQuery `on` method to attach an event handler to all `anchor` child elements of the element whose ID is `territories`. The event handler then saves the selected territory ID to the hidden field inside the form we created earlier.

Modal dialogs

Modals are used to provide a pop-up dialog style element that can be used to provide information to the user or even allow the user to complete a form inside the modal. A Bootstrap modal is essentially made of three parts: a header, body, and footer. You can put any standard HTML markup inside the modal's `body` element, including standard text or even an embedded YouTube video.

As a general rule, always place the modal's markup in a top-level position inside your view—the top or bottom of the view is the best place to put your modal markup.

Using the following HTML and Razor markup, we'll create a modal that prompts the user whether they would like to continue deleting a certain customer record from the database. We'll declare a `<form>` element inside the modal's body and use a button that is created inside the modal's footer element to submit the form. We'll also create a button that the user can click on to dismiss the modal. This is accomplished by adding the `data-dismiss="modal"` attribute to the button as follows:

```
<div class="modal fade" id="deleteConfirmationModal" tabindex="-1"
role="dialog" aria-hidden="true">
    <div class="modal-dialog">
        <div class="modal-content">
            <div class="modal-header">
                <button type="button" class="close" data-
                dismiss="modal" aria-hidden="true">&times;</button>
                <h4 class="modal-title">Deletion confirmation</h4>
```

```
            </div>
            <div class="modal-body">
                <p>You're about to delete the customer
                '@Model.CompanyName'. </p>
                <p>
                    <strong>Are you sure you want to continue?
                    </strong>
                </p>
                @using (Html.BeginForm("Delete", "Customers",
                FormMethod.Post, new { @id = "delete-form",
                role = "form" }))
                {
                    @Html.HiddenFor(m => m.CustomerId)
                    @Html.AntiForgeryToken()
                }
            </div>
            <div class="modal-footer">
                <button type="button" class="btn btn-default"
                onclick="$('#delete-form').submit();">Yes,
                delete this customer.</button>
                <button type="button" class="btn btn-primary"
                data-dismiss="modal">No, do not delete.</button>
            </div>
        </div>
    </div>
</div>
```

The form is submitted to the `Delete` action inside `CustomerController`. The code for this method is as follows:

```
[HttpPost, ValidateAntiForgeryToken]
public ActionResult Delete(int customerId)
{
    var model = _context.Customers.FirstOrDefault(i =>
    i.CustomerId == customerId);
    if (model != null)
    {
        _context.Customers.Remove(model);
        _context.SaveChanges();
        return RedirectToAction("Index").WithSuccess("Customer
        (" + model.CompanyName + ") deleted.");
    }
    return RedirectToAction("Index").WithError("Customer was
    not found.");
}
```

In order to show the modal, we do not need to write any JavaScript. We can simply add a `data-toggle="modal"` attribute to the `anchor` or `button` element that should show the modal when the user clicks on it, as illustrated in the following code:

```
<a href="#" data-toggle="modal" data-target="#deleteConfirmationModal
">Delete</a>
```

To indicate which modal to show, we specify the ID of the modal inside the `data-target` attribute.

The result of the aforementioned code will display a modal similar to the one illustrated in the following screenshot:

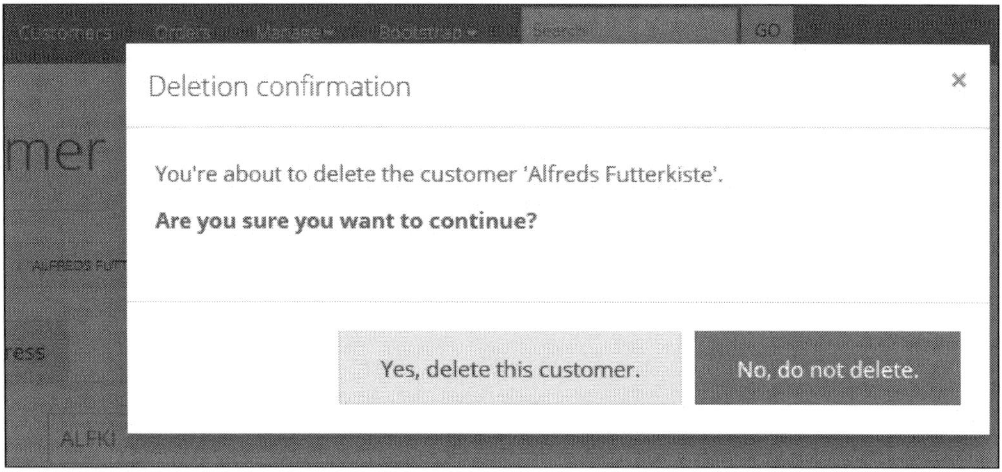

You also have the option to not use the `data-` API to show the modal, using jQuery to show and hide the modal. The following JavaScript shows the modal which ID is set to `deleteConfirmationModal` when the page loads:

```
$(document).ready(function () {
    $('#deleteConfirmationModal').modal('show');
});
```

You can also use the same function in order to hide the modal:

```
$('#deleteConfirmationModal').modal('hide');
```

Tabs

Tabs provide an option to split your content into separate pages. This is an ideal component when you have a particularly large form, which you want to split up into a logical grouping. For example, when you're editing a customer's record, you might want to split their contact details from their address details, as illustrated in the following screenshot:

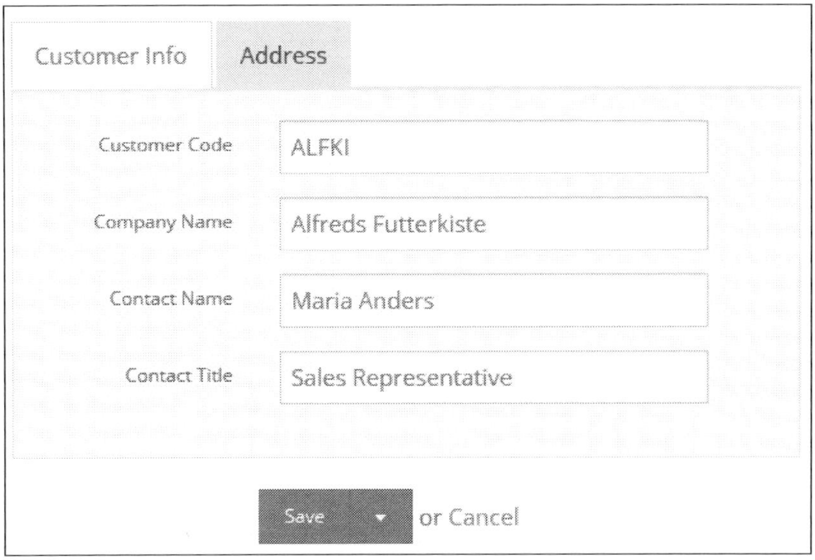

Bootstrap tabs are divided into two parts. You first need to specify the tab names and the ID of the corresponding `<div>` element to show when the user clicks on the tab. This is done by creating a standard unordered list `<ul>` element with the tab names as child list items `<li>`. The `<ul>` element's class must be set to `nav nav-tabs` or `nav nav-pills`, as illustrated in the following script:

```
<ul class="nav nav-tabs">
    <li class="active"><a href="#info" data-toggle="tab">Customer
    Info</a></li>
    <li><a href="#address" data-toggle="tab">Address</a></li>
</ul>
```

You can use a tab or pill navigation by setting the `<li>` element's `data-toggle` attribute to either `tab` or `pill` and setting the `<ul>` element's class to `nav-pills`. The result will look like the following screenshot in your browser:

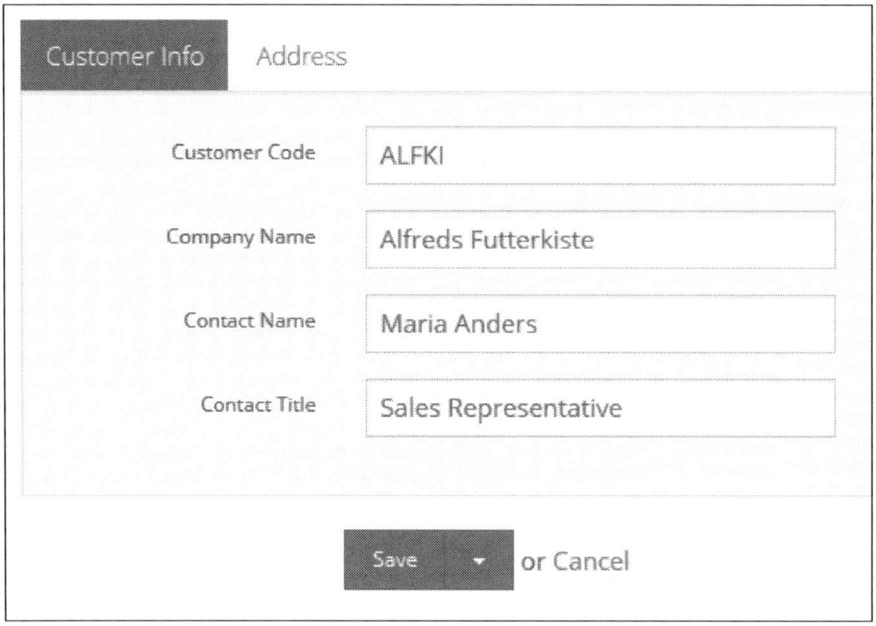

To specify the content for the tabs, create a new `<div>` element and set its class to `tab-content`. Create a `<div>` element for each tab inside the parent `<div>` element and set each tab's `<div>` element's class to `tab-pane` as follows:

```
<div class="tab-content well">
    <div class="tab-pane active" id="info">
        Info Tab Content goes here
    </div>
    <div class="tab-pane" id="address">
        Address Tab Content goes here
    </div>
</div>
```

In the preceding markup, we created two tabs and set the `active` tab to the `info` tab by setting its class to `active`.

You can also activate a specific page using jQuery. To activate the `address` tab as soon as the page loads, use the following code:

```
$(document).ready(function () {
    $('.nav-tabs a[href="#address"]').tab('show');
});
```

Tooltips

Bootstrap's tooltip plugin is an updated version of Jason Frame's jQuery.tipsy plugin. Tooltips can be used to provide users with additional information labels about specific content on your pages or provide insight into what input is expected in form elements.

Tooltips can be used on a variety of elements; for example, the following markup shows a tooltip when a user hovers over an anchor `<a>` element:

```
<a data-toggle="tooltip" data-placement="top" data-original-
title="Welcome to the wonderful World of Grammar!" href="#" >World of
Grammar</a>
```

To use a tooltip on any element, add a `data-toggle="tooltip"` attribute to it. You can specify the placement of the tooltip by setting the `data-placement` attribute to one of the following values:

- `top`
- `bottom`
- `left`
- `right`

Finally, set the value of the `data-original-title` attribute to specify what text should be shown inside the tooltip.

One caveat of tooltips is that because of performance concerns, the `data-` API is opt-in, which means you have to initialize the plugin manually. To do this, add the following JavaScript to your page:

```
<script type="text/javascript">
    $(document).ready(function () {
        $('[data-toggle="tooltip"]').tooltip();
    });
</script>
```

The preceding code finds all elements whose `data-toggle` attribute is set to `tooltip` and initializes the tooltip plugin for these elements. The result will look similar to the following screenshot in your browser:

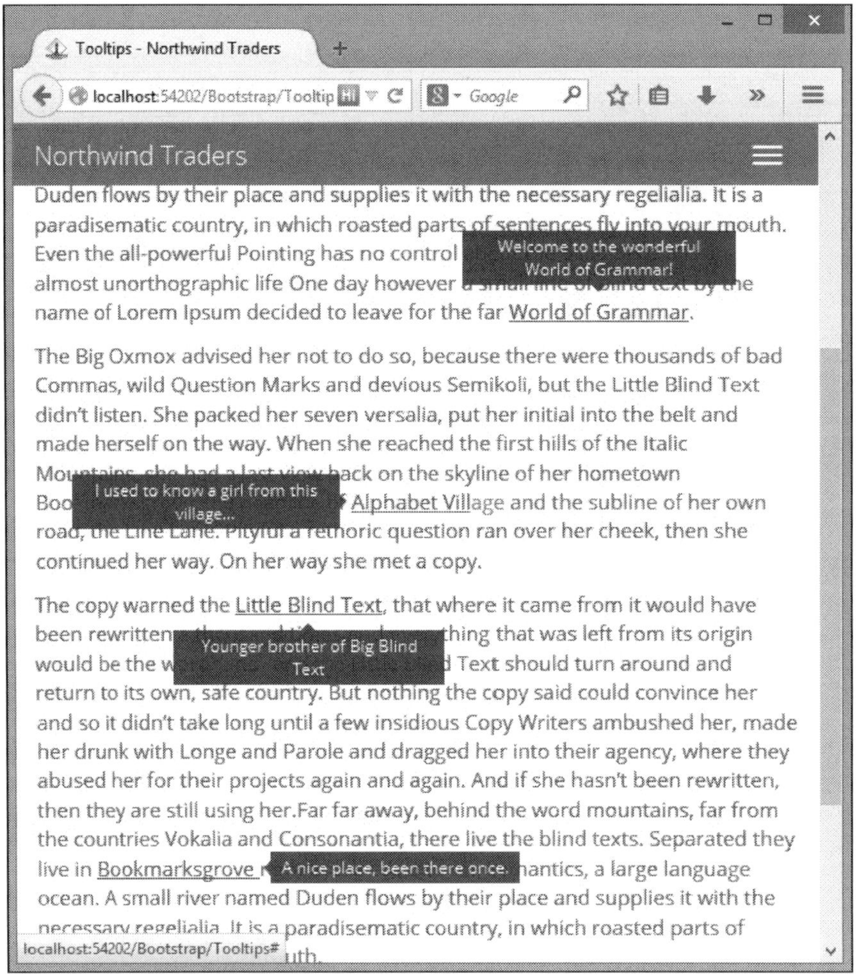

Popovers

Popovers are similar to tooltips due to the fact that they can provide users with additional information about an element, but they are designed to show a little more content, as popovers also allow you to display a header.

Popovers are defined in a similar fashion in which you would define a popup by adding the `data-toggle`, `data-placement`, `data-original-title`, and `data-content` attributes to an element. The following markup displays a popup when a user clicks on an anchor `<a>` element:

```
<a data-content="The protagonist of Franz Kafka's short story The
Metamorphosis" data-placement="bottom" title="" data-toggle="popover"
href="#" data-original-title="From Wikipedia">Gregor Samsa</a>
```

Setting the `data-toggle` attribute to `popover` specifies to the plugin that it needs to show a popover. The `data-content` attribute contains the content that will be shown inside the popover, and the `data-original-title` attribute sets the title of the popover. The `data-placement` attribute indicates the placement of the popover and supports four values, which include `top`, `bottom`, `left`, and `right`.

You can also specify the trigger that will show the popover by setting the `data-trigger` attribute's value. Popovers can be triggered when a user clicks or hovers over the element or when the element has focus. You can also specify that the trigger should be activated manually. The four options for the `data-trigger` attribute are `click`, `hover`, `focus`, and `manual`.

As with tooltips, the `data-` API is an opt-in, so you would need to initialize the popover plugin manually. In the following code, using jQuery, we'll find all elements on a page whose `data-toggle` attribute is set to `popover` and initialize the popover plugin for each one:

```
<script type="text/javascript">
    $(document).ready(function () {
        $('[data-toggle="popover"]').popover();
    });
</script>
```

The popover plugin will appear similar to the following screenshot in your browser:

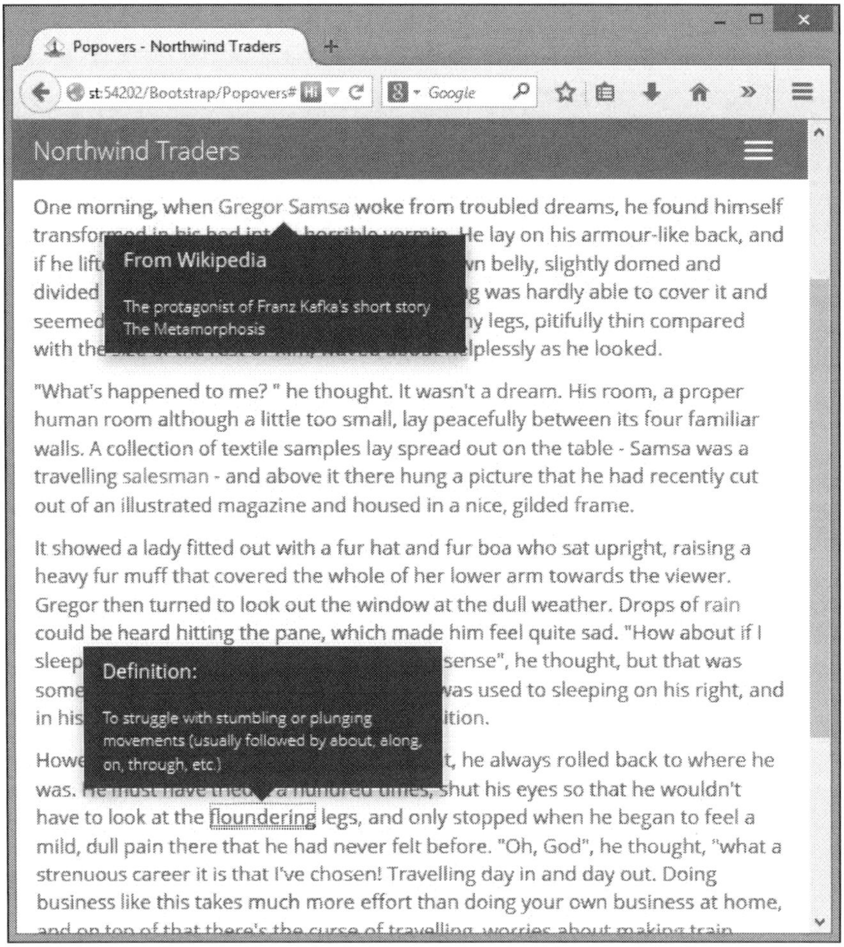

The accordion component

The accordion component is probably best known for FAQ pages or pages that require a lot of content that is broken down into manageable parts. An accordion is made up of a number of panel groups. Each panel group, in turn, has a heading and body elements. To use the accordion component in our project, perform the following steps:

1. To allow the panel to collapse when the user clicks on its heading, we need to add a `data-toggle` attribute to an anchor `<a>` element inside the `panel` heading element and set its value to `collapse`.

2. We also need to specify the parent element of the panel by setting the `data-parent` attribute's value to the ID of the parent panel group. Next, set the `anchor` element's `href` attribute to the ID of the `<div>` element that contains the content.
3. Finally, we also need to set the `panel` body element's class to `panel-collapse collapse`. In the following code, we'll create an accordion component that contains two panel groups. The first panel group is automatically visible when the page loads because we'll set its class to `panel-collapse collapse in`:

```
<div class="panel-group" id="accordion">
    <div class="panel panel-default">
        <div class="panel-heading">
            <h4 class="panel-title">
                <a data-toggle="collapse" data-parent="#accordion"
                href="#questionOne">
                    How do I order from you?
                </a>
            </h4>
        </div>
        <div id="questionOne" class="panel-collapse collapse in">
            <div class="panel-body">
                Mauris egestas sem a ante accumsan tincidunt.
                Vivamus id nisl vulputate, placerat arcu et.
                sapien.
            </div>
        </div>
    </div>

    <div class="panel panel-default">
        <div class="panel-heading">
            <h4 class="panel-title">
                <a data-toggle="collapse" data-parent="#accordion"
                href="#questionTwo">
                    Do you ship internationally?
                </a>
            </h4>
        </div>
        <div id="questionTwo" class="panel-collapse collapse">
            <div class="panel-body">
                Integer aliquet ligula eget elit faucibus, quis
                pretium justo iaculis. Quisque quis dolor
                volutpat, varius tellus eget, luctus nibh.
                Cras tempus tincidunt.
            </div>
        </div>
    </div>
</div>
```

4. The accordion should look similar to the following screenshot:

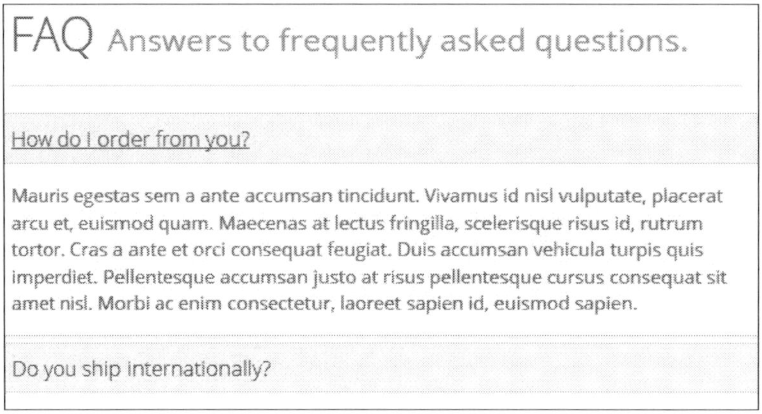

The carousel component

The carousel component is a user interface element, which you'll see on a number of websites. It is essentially a slideshow that cycles through different elements, usually images. The carousel component should be contained inside a `<div>` element with a class name of `carousel` and a `data-ride` attribute with a value of `carousel`. To use the carousel component in your project, perform the following steps:

1. The carousel component consists of an ordered list element, `<ol>`, that renders as small circles in the browser and indicates which slide is currently active. The markup for this element is as follows:

```
<ol class="carousel-indicators">
    <li data-target="#myCarousel" data-slide-to="0"
    class="active"></li>
    <li data-target="#myCarousel" data-slide-to="1"></li>
    <li data-target="#myCarousel" data-slide-to="2"></li>
</ol>
```

2. Next, another `<div>` element with a class name of `carousel-inner` needs to be created. This element will contain the actual slides and their content. The following markup creates such an element with one slide:

```
<div class="carousel-inner">
    <div class="item active">
```

```
                <img src="@Url.Content("~/Images/slide1.jpg")"
                alt="First slide">
                <div class="container">
                    <div class="carousel-caption">
                        <h1>Unto all said together great in
                        image.</h1>
                        <p>Won't saw light to void brought fifth
was brought god abundantly for you waters life seasons he after
replenish beast. Creepeth beginning.</p>
                        <p><a class="btn btn-lg btn-primary"
                        href="#" role="button">Read more</a></p>
                    </div>
                </div>
            </div>
</div>
```

3. Finally, to add arrows on either side of the carousel to indicate to the user that they can navigate to the next slide, add the following markup to the parent `<div>` element:

```
<a class="left carousel-control" href="#myCarousel" data-
slide="prev"><span class="glyphicon glyphicon-chevron-left"></
span></a>
<a class="right carousel-control" href="#myCarousel" data-
slide="next"><span class="glyphicon glyphicon-chevron-right"></
span></a>
```

4. The duration for which each slide should be shown can be set via the `data-interval` attribute. In the following markup, we set the interval between slides to be `10` seconds:

```
<div id="myCarousel" class="carousel" data-ride="carousel"
data-interval="10000">
```

5. As with all the other plugins, you also have a choice of initializing the plugin and setting its options using JavaScript. In the following code, we'll initialize the carousel and set the interval between slides to `10` seconds:

```
$('#myCarousel').carousel({
  interval: 10000
})
```

Summary

In this chapter, we examined various Bootstrap JavaScript plugins, how to initialize them, and how to set their options using either the `data-` API or the programmatic JavaScript approach.

In the next chapter, we'll explore how you can create your own ASP.NET MVC helpers to reduce the amount of HTML markup you have to write in order to create a number of Bootstrap elements and components.

5

Creating ASP.NET MVC Bootstrap Helpers

ASP.NET MVC allows developers to create their own HTML helper methods either by creating static or extension methods. In essence, an HTML helper is simply a method that returns an HTML string.

HTML helpers enable you to use the same common block of markup on multiple pages and make the code and markup in your pages easier to read and maintain. This promotes the use of reusable code, and developers can also unit test their helper methods.

In this chapter, we will cover the following topics:

- An overview of the built-in ASP.NET MVC HTML helpers
- Creating helpers using the `@helper` syntax
- Creating HTML helpers using static methods
- Creating HTML helper extension methods
- Creating fluent HTML helpers
- Creating self-closing helpers

Built-in HTML helpers

An `HtmlHelper` is a method that renders HTML content inside a view. It is intended to allow developers to reuse a common block of HTML markup across multiple pages.

ASP.NET MVC provides a range of standard, out-of-the-box HTML helpers. For example, to produce the following HTML for a textbox with an ID and name attribute of `CustomerName`, use the following code:

```
<input type="text" name="CustomerName" id="CustomerName">
```

You should use the `TextBox` helper as illustrated in the following code:

```
@Html.TextBox("CustomerName")
```

Majority of the built-in HTML helpers offer several overloaded versions. For instance, to create a textbox and explicitly set its name and value attributes, you should use the following overloaded `TextBox` helper method:

```
@Html.TextBox("CustomerName"","Northwind Traders")
```

Most built-in helpers also offer the option to specify HTML attributes for the element that is generated by passing in an anonymous type. In the following example, we'll create a textbox and set its `style` property using one of the overload methods:

```
@Html.TextBox("CustomerName","Northwind Traders", new {
style="background-color:Blue;" })
```

> You can read more about the standard HTML helpers available in ASP.NET MVC at `http://bit.ly/MVCFormHelpers`.

Creating a custom helper

As Bootstrap offers a variety of different components, it lends itself perfectly towards the use of helpers. The simplest form of helper in ASP.NET MVC is the one that you can create using the `@helper` syntax. A custom helper can include any HTML or even Razor markup. To create a simple helper method to generate a Bootstrap button, complete the following steps:

1. Create a new folder called `App_Code` inside the root folder of your website.
2. Create a new file called `BootstrapHelpers.cshtml` inside the newly created `App_Code` folder.
3. Add the following code to the `BootstrapHelper.cshtml` file:

```
@helper PrimaryButtonSmall(string id,string caption)
{
  <button id="@id" type="button" class="btn btn-primary btn-sm">@
caption</button>
}
```

This code employs the `@helper` syntax to create a new helper called `PrimaryButtonSmall`. The helper accepts two parameters in order to specify the `id` attribute of the `button` element as well as the button's `caption` element. We've added appropriate Bootstrap classes to the `button` element in order to render a blue primary button. Any custom helper must reside inside the `App_Code` folder in order for ASP.NET MVC to recognize it inside your view.

Using a helper in a view

Let's use the helper we just created in the preceding section. To do this, open a view in your site, and add the following code to the page:

```
@BootstrapHelpers.PrimaryButtonSmall("myButton","My New Button")
```

When you run the site and view the source of the page on which the helper is used, you'll see that the helper generated the correct HTML markup to create the following primary Bootstrap button:

```
<button class="btn btn-primary btn-sm" type="button" id="myButton">My
New Button</button>
```

You'll notice that although this approach works, it is not practical because it means we would have to create an HTML helper for each style and size of button available. A possible solution to this problem is to change our helper code in order to accept a parameter with which the developer can specify which style and size the button should be. To accomplish this, perform the following steps:

1. Open the `BootstrapHelpers.cshtml` file that is located inside the `App_Code` folder.
2. Replace the code inside the file with the following code:

   ```
   @helper Button(string style, string size, string caption, string
   id)
   {
       <button id="@id" type="button" class="btn btn-@style btn-@
   size">@caption</button>
   }
   ```

3. Open the view that uses the helper and add the following markup:

   ```
   @BootstrapHelpers.Button("danger","lg","A Large
   button","myLargeButton")
   ```

   In the preceding step, we've updated our helper to accept two string parameters to specify the size and style of the Bootstrap button. The problem with this approach is that the developer still needs to know the name of the style and size in order to render the correct button.

Creating helpers using static methods

The easiest alternative to creating helpers using the `@helper` syntax we mentioned earlier is to create static methods that simply return a string that contains an HTML markup.

In order to accomplish this, we need to complete the following steps:

1. Create a new folder called `Helpers` inside the root folder of your project.
2. Add a new class to this folder called `Enums.cs`. This file will contain all the enumerators for our project.
3. Add the following code to the `Enums.cs` file:

```
public class Enums
{
    public enum ButtonStyle
    {
        Default,
        Primary,
        Success,
        Info,
        Warning,
        Danger,
        Link
    }

    public enum ButtonSize
    {
        Large,
        Small,
        ExtraSmall,
        Normal
    }
}
```

4. Create a new class called `ButtonHelper.cs` in the `Helpers` folder.
5. Add a method called `Button` to the `ButtonHelper` class, and add the following code to it:

```
public static MvcHtmlString Button(string caption, Enums.
ButtonStyle style, Enums.ButtonSize size)
{
    if (size != Enums.ButtonSize.Normal)
    {
        return new MvcHtmlString(string.Format("<button
type=\"button\" class=\"btn btn-{0} btn-{1}\">{2}</button>",
style.ToString().ToLower(), ToBootstrapSize(size), caption));
```

```
    }
    return new MvcHtmlString(string.Format("<button
type=\"button\" class=\"btn btn-{0}\">{1}</button>", style.
ToString().ToLower(), caption));
}
```

6. Finally, add another method called `ToBootstrapSize`:

```
private static string ToBootstrapSize(Enums.ButtonSize size)
{
    string bootstrapSize = string.Empty;
    switch (size)
    {
        case Enums.ButtonSize.Large:
            bootstrapSize = "lg";
            break;

        case Enums.ButtonSize.Small:
            bootstrapSize = "sm";
            break;

        case Enums.ButtonSize.ExtraSmall:
            bootstrapSize = "xs";
            break;
    }
    return bootstrapSize;
}
```

The `Button` method we created earlier accepts three parameters in order to set the button's caption, size, and style. We use the enumerator values declared in the `Enums.cs` file in order to list the available sizes and styles for the button—this releases the developer from memorizing the exact Bootstrap class names for each.

The `Button` method returns an `MvcHtmlString` object, which was introduced in .NET 4. The `MvcHtmlString` object represents an HTML-encoded string, which does not need to be encoded again. If we simply return a normal string object, the actual HTML would be rendered inside the view instead of the button.

The `ToBootstrapSize` method basically converts the `ButtonSize` value to a valid Bootstrap class name that represents the size of the button. The result will look similar to the following screenshot in the browser:

Using the static method helper in a view

In order to use the static method helper we created earlier, open the view you intend to use it in, and add the following Razor markup to it:

```
@ButtonHelper.Button("My Button",Enums.ButtonStyle.Warning, Enums.
ButtonSize.Normal)
```

In order to use the helper, you will need to include a reference to its namespace at the top of your view by adding the following `using` statement:

```
@using Northwind.Web.Helpers
```

Creating helpers using extension methods

If we want our helpers to behave in a manner similar to the built-in ASP.NET MVC HTML helpers, we need to create an extension method. Extension methods are a technique used to add new methods to an existing class.

> Extension methods are a very powerful and intuitive approach to add additional functionality to existing classes and can help you in many ways. You can read more about extension methods on MSDN at `http://bit.ly/ExtMethods`.

We'll create an extension method to the `HtmlHelper` class that is represented by a view's HTML property by completing the following steps:

1. Start by adding a new class file called `ButtonExtensions.cs` to the `Helpers` folder in the root of your project.
2. Change the class type to `static`. Extension methods need to be declared inside a static class.
3. Add a new method called `BootstrapButton` to the class. The first parameter of the method indicates which class the extension extends and must be preceded with the `this` keyword.
4. The remaining parameters will be used to specify the caption, style, and size of the button. The code for the method is as follows:

   ```
   public static MvcHtmlString BootstrapButton(this HtmlHelper
   helper, string caption, Enums.ButtonStyle style, Enums.ButtonSize
   size)
   {
       if (size != Enums.ButtonSize.Normal)
   ```

```
    {
        return new MvcHtmlString(string.Format("<button
type=\"button\" class=\"btn btn-{0} btn-{1}\">{2}</button>",
style.ToString().ToLower(), ToBootstrapSize(size), caption));
    }
    return new MvcHtmlString(string.Format("<button
type=\"button\" class=\"btn btn-{0}\">{1}</button>", style.
ToString().ToLower(), caption));
}
```

The `BootstrapButton` method is the same as the `Button` method in the `ButtonHelper` class we created earlier, apart from the fact that it is an extension to the `HtmlHelper` object.

Using the extension method helper in a view

As the `BootstrapButton` method is an extension method, using it involves opening the view and adding the following markup to it:

```
@Html.BootstrapButton("My Button", Enums.ButtonStyle.Info, Enums.
ButtonSize.Normal)
```

Note that we're using the standard HTML helper to invoke the `BootstrapButton` method.

Creating fluent HTML helpers

Fluent interfaces is a technique used in software development to implement an object-orientated API in such a manner that it provides more readable code, and it is usually implemented using method chaining.

> The term "fluent interface" was first used by Eric Evans and Martin Fowler. If you'd like to learn more about fluent interfaces, read Martin Fowler's blog post available at `http://bit.ly/FluentInterfaces`.

We'll create an HTML helper that will help us render Bootstrap alerts with a single line of code. The helper will take a fluent interface approach, which means that we'll be able to render a dismissible, warning alert box using the following line of code:

```
@Html.Alert("This is a warning").Warning().Dismissible()
```

To create fluent HTML helpers, complete the following steps:

1. Create a new subfolder called `Alerts` inside the `Helpers` folder in your project.
2. Add a new interface to the `Alerts` folder called `IAlertFluent`. The interface should implement the `IHtmlString` interface.
3. Add a new `IAlertFluent` property called `Dismissible` to the interface. The code for the `IAlertFluent` interface should represent the following:

```
public interface IAlertFluent : IHtmlString
{
    IAlertFluent Dismissible(bool canDismiss = true);
}
```

4. Next, add a new interface to the `Alerts` folder called `IAlert`, and add four `IAlertFluent` properties called `Danger`, `Info`, `Success`, and `Warning`. These four properties will be used to set the `Alert` style as follows:

```
public interface IAlert : IAlertFluent
{
    IAlertFluent Danger();
    IAlertFluent Info();
    IAlertFluent Success();
    IAlertFluent Warning();
}
```

5. Next, we'll need to add a class that implements the `IAlert` interface. Add a new class called `Alert.cs` to the `Alerts` folder.
6. Before we can implement the methods on the `Alert` class, we need to create a class that will implement the `IAlertFluent` interface. Now, add a new class called `AlertFluent.cs` to the `Alerts` folder.
7. The `IAlertFluent` interface only specifies one method, so we'll implement it in the `AlertFluent` class and create a constructor that accepts an `Alert` object as a parameter as follows:

```
public class AlertFluent : IAlertFluent
{
    private readonly Alert _parent;

    public AlertFluent(Alert parent)
    {
        _parent = parent;
    }
```

```
    public IAlertFluent Dismissible(bool canDismiss = true)
    {
        return _parent.Dismissible(canDismiss);
    }

    public string ToHtmlString()
    {
        return _parent.ToHtmlString();
    }
}
```

8. Open the `Enum.cs` file, and add a new enumerator called `AlertStyle`:

```
public enum AlertStyle
{
    Danger,
    Info,
    Success,
    Warning,
}
```

9. Open the `Alert.cs` file, and add a local `AlertStyle` enum field called `_style`, a Boolean field called `_dismissible`, and a string called `_message`.
10. Next, implement each of the methods that the `IAlert` interface specifies. Each method will set the `_style` property and return a new instance of the `AlertFluent` object. A reference to the `Alert` class is passed to the `AlertFluent` constructor as a parameter. The code for each is indicated as follows:

```
public IAlertFluent Danger()
{
    _style=Enums.AlertStyle.Danger;
    return new AlertFluent(this);
}

public IAlertFluent Info()
{
    _style = Enums.AlertStyle.Info;
    return new AlertFluent(this);
}

public IAlertFluent Success()
{
    _style = Enums.AlertStyle.Success;
    return new AlertFluent(this);
}
```

```
public IAlertFluent Warning()
{
    _style = Enums.AlertStyle.Warning;
    return new AlertFluent(this);
}
```

11. The `Dismissible` method works in a similar fashion; it sets the local `_dismissible` field and returns a new instance of the `AlertFluent` object:

```
public IAlertFluent Dismissible(bool canDismiss = true)
{
    this._dismissible = canDismiss;
    return new AlertFluent(this);
}
```

12. Finally, we need to implement the `ToHtmlString` property. This property is specified in the `IHtmlString` interface. We'll use the `TagBuilder` object to construct the HTML markup for the Bootstrap `Alert` class. The code for the `ToHtmlString` method is as follows:

```
public string ToHtmlString()
{
    var alertDiv = new TagBuilder("div");
    alertDiv.AddCssClass("alert");
    alertDiv.AddCssClass("alert-" + _style.ToString().ToLower());
    alertDiv.InnerHtml = _message;

    if (_dismissible)
    {
        alertDiv.AddCssClass("alert-dismissible");
        alertDiv.InnerHtml += AddCloseButton();
    }

    return alertDiv.ToString();
}
```

13. The preceding code creates a new `<div>` element and adds the necessary Bootstrap `Alert` classes to it. It then checks whether the alert should be dismissible, and if so, adds the appropriate class and generates the HTML to show a `close` button by calling the `AddCloseButton` method:

```
private static TagBuilder AddCloseButton()
{
    var closeButton = new TagBuilder("button");
    closeButton.AddCssClass("close");
```

```
        closeButton.Attributes.Add("data-dismiss", "alert");
        closeButton.InnerHtml = "&times;";
        return closeButton;
    }
```

14. The `AddCloseButton` method also uses the `TagBuilder` object to build up the HTML needed in order to render a `close` button inside the Bootstrap `Alert` class.

Using the fluent HTML helper in a view

In order to use the fluent HTML helper inside a view, we need to add one final file called `AlertHelper.cs` to the `Alerts` folder. This class will add an extension method to the `HtmlHelper` object in order to render a Bootstrap `Alert` class. Add a new method called `Alert` to the class. This method should return an `Alert` object, and it will accept two parameters. The first parameter must be preceded with the `this` keyword and is used to indicate which class the extension will extend. The second parameter will be the actual text that will be displayed inside the Bootstrap `Alert` class.

The code for the `Alert` class is as follows:

```
public static class AlertHelper
{
    public static Alert Alert(this HtmlHelper html,string message)
    {
        return new Alert(message);
    }
}
```

Open a view and add the following markup to render a dismissible Bootstrap alert that will display a danger-styled message:

```
@Html.Alert("Core meltdown imminent").Danger().Dismissible()
```

The alert will look similar to the following screenshot in the browser:

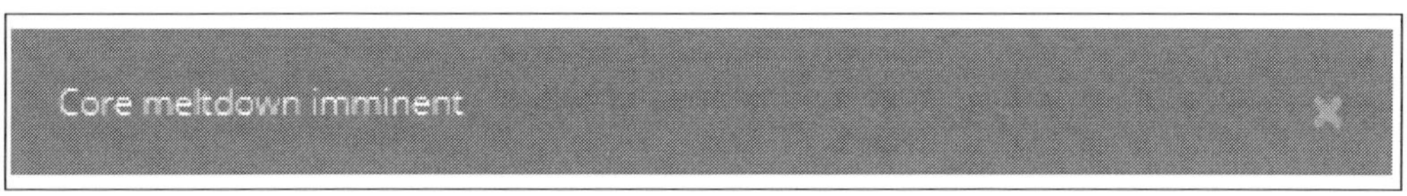

Creating self-closing helpers

Self-closing helpers are helpers that can contain HTML and Razor markup. The built-in `@Html.BeginForm()` helper is an example of this type of helper.

In order to create this type of HTML helper, we'll need to create a helper class that implements the `IDisposable` interface. Using the `IDisposable` interface, we can write the element's closing tags when the object is disposed.

The Bootstrap `Panel` component is a perfect candidate for such a helper. To create the helper, we'll have to complete the following steps:

1. Create a new subfolder called `Panels` inside the `Helpers` folder in your project.
2. Open the `Enums.cs` file, and add a new item called `PanelStyle`:

   ```
   public enum PanelStyle
   {
       Default,
       Primary,
       Success,
       Info,
       Warning,
       Danger
   }
   ```

3. Add a new class file called `Panel.cs` to the `Panels` folder.
4. Add a new private read-only field to the class called `_writer`.
5. Create a constructor for the `Panel` class that accepts three parameters. The first is a reference to the `HtmlHelper` object, the second specifies the title of the panel, and the third indicates the style of the panel.
6. Add the following code to the `Panel` class's constructor method:

   ```
   public Panel(HtmlHelper helper, string title, Enums.PanelStyle
   style = Enums.PanelStyle.Default)
   {
       _writer = helper.ViewContext.Writer;

       var panelDiv = new TagBuilder("div");
       panelDiv.AddCssClass("panel-" + style.ToString().ToLower());
       panelDiv.AddCssClass("panel");

       var panelHeadingDiv = new TagBuilder("div");
       panelHeadingDiv.AddCssClass("panel-heading");
   ```

```
        var heading3Div = new TagBuilder("h3");
        heading3Div.AddCssClass("panel-title");
        heading3Div.SetInnerText(title);

        var panelBodyDiv = new TagBuilder("div");
        panelBodyDiv.AddCssClass("panel-body");

        panelHeadingDiv.InnerHtml = heading3Div.ToString();

        string html = string.Format("{0}{1}{2}", panelDiv.
    ToString(TagRenderMode.StartTag), panelHeadingDiv, panelBodyDiv.
    ToString(TagRenderMode.StartTag));
        _writer.Write(html);
    }
```

In this code, we've set the `_writer` field to the `Writer` property of the `HtmlHelper` objects' `ViewContext` property. By utilizing this property, we'll be able to write HTML to the current view.

We then built up the `panel` element's HTML markup using the `TagBuilder` object and finally, sent the result to the `_writer` object to output. Note that we used the overloaded `ToString` method of `TagBuilder` in order to specify that it should only generate the starting tags of the `<div>` element.

The two `<div>` elements with class names `panel` and `panel-body` will be closed in the `Panel` class's `Dispose` method, which is implemented in the following manner:

```
public void Dispose()
{
    _writer.Write("</div></div>");
}
```

Using the self-closing helper in a view

To use the helper we created earlier in our view, we'll use the C# `using` keyword. The `using` keyword restricts the scope of an object and thus, works well with the `IDisposable` interface. In essence, as soon as the helper has finished rendering its HTML output, the `Dispose` method will automatically be invoked, thus closing the last two `<div>` element tags.

To use the helper in a view, use the following markup:

```
@using (Html.Panel("Title", Enums.PanelStyle.Success))
{
    <p>Hello World</p>
    <p>Lorem ipsum dolor sit amet, consectetur adipiscing elit.</p>
}
```

The helper will generate the required HTML in order to show the following panel in the browser:

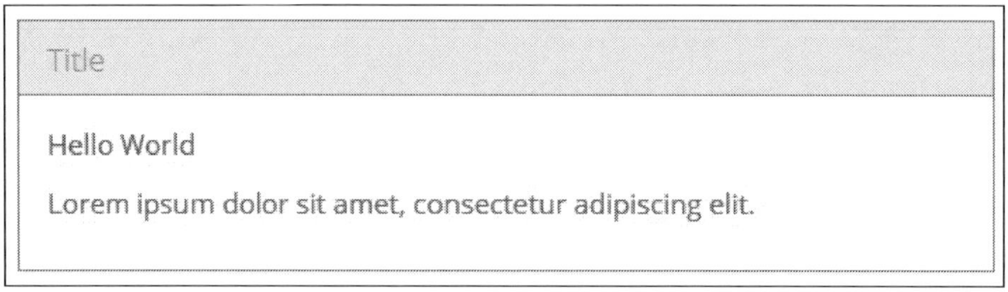

Summary

In this chapter, we explored how you can decrease the amount of markup in your views, using HTML helpers. We also looked at how you can write helpers that will enable developers who are not familiar with the Bootstrap framework to use helpers to add styled components to their views.

In the next chapter, we'll dive into generating scaffolded views that are correctly styled using the Bootstrap styles and layouts.

6
Creating T4 Templates to Scaffold Bootstrap Views

The ASP.NET MVC framework relies on scaffolding to generate most of what you need for an ASP.NET MVC including views and controllers. The standard scaffolding templates would suffice for most projects, but there will be cases where you would require finer grain control over the code that is generated.

Visual Studio uses T4 templates internally to generate many of the item templates available, and developers are also able to harness this functionality in their own projects.

In this chapter, we will explore the following topics:

- An overview of scaffolding
- T4 templates
- Tools available for making the use of T4 easier
- A brief overview of the T4 syntax
- Customizing the generated code for controllers and views
- Creating a custom scaffolder

An overview of scaffolding

Scaffolding is a system used by many development frameworks, including ASP.NET MVC, to generate a basic view and controller code for database operations such as create, read, update, and delete.

Visual Studio 2013 already includes code generators for ASP.NET MVC and Web API projects, and using these built-in scaffolding templates can drastically reduce the amount of time you spend on creating standard views and controller actions. When adding a standard controller to an ASP.NET MVC project in Visual Studio 2013, you're already using scaffolding, and this is indicated by the fact that the dialog window used to add a new controller's caption is **Add Scaffold**:

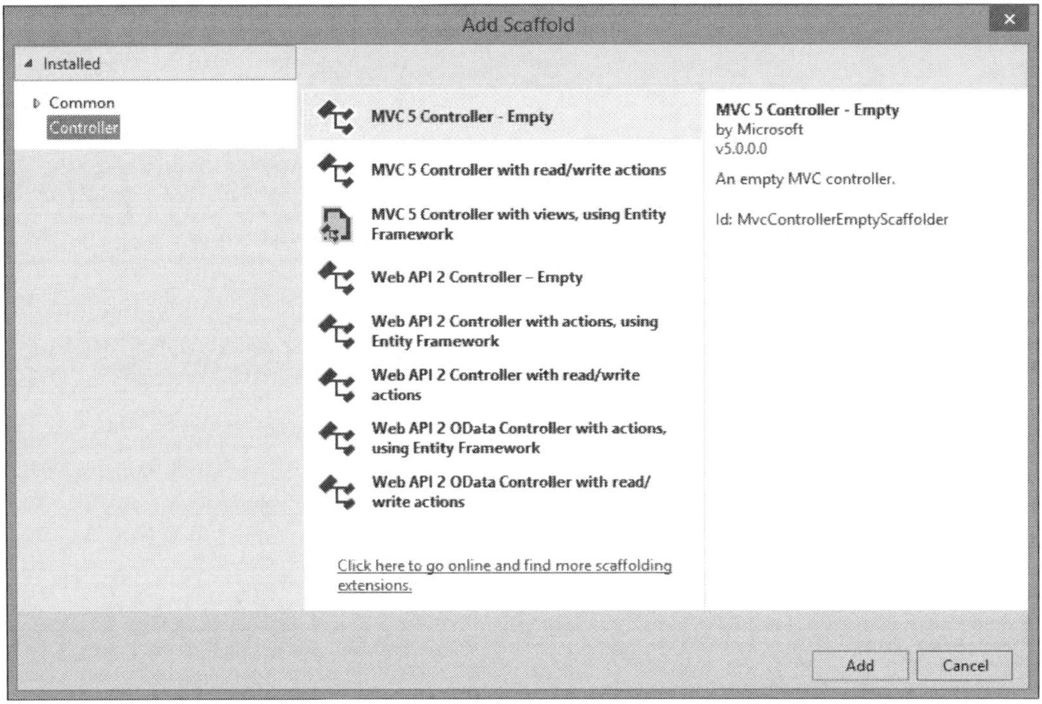

T4 templates

T4 stands for Text Template Transformation Toolkit, which is Microsoft's template-based text-generation framework. T4 is a combination of control logic and text blocks, which can generate any type of text file, including C# or VB source files.

The T4 code generator is built into Visual Studio and is used to generate the built-in ASP.NET MVC templates, including the standard MVC and Web API controller templates.

> Oleg Sych wrote a number of very informative blog posts on how to use T4 templates and how to get optimal results by using it in your own development project. To read more, you can visit his blog at `http://bit.ly/OlegSychT4`.

Unfortunately, Visual Studio does not provide syntax highlighting or intelliSense support when editing T4 templates, but there are free tools available that can add these features to Visual Studio for you.

T4 tools

Since Visual Studio does not provide T4 intelliSense by default, we'll need to install a third-party extension to enable this functionality for us. Fortunately, there are two free alternatives available. These are as follows:

- The Devart T4 editor for Visual Studio (`http://bit.ly/DevArtT4`)
- The tangible T4 editor (`http://bit.ly/TangibleT4`)

Both these extensions provide similar functionalities, but for the T4 examples in this book, we'll use the tangible T4 editor.

Another free extension that is vital in making the creation of T4 templates much easier is the **SideWaffle** extension for Visual Studio. SideWaffle will add a number of extremely-useful item templates to Visual Studio, which we'll use to build our own ASP.NET MVC scaffolded views. You can download SideWaffle from `http://www.sidewaffle.com/`.

> SideWaffle not only provides item templates for T4, but also offers a range of project and item templates as well as a host of very useful snippets. It is an actively-maintained open source project on GitHub and an indispensable tool for any .NET developer.

The T4 syntax

T4 templates have a very specific syntax, which can appear somewhat daunting, but once you get used to it, it is relatively simple to understand and use. T4 uses three distinct tags to indicate code blocks.

The first code block is `<#= #>` and is used to execute the code within the tag and will return a text result. For example, in the following markup, the code will return the value in the `ViewName` variable inside the T4 template:

```
<#= ViewName #>
```

The `<# #>` code block executes the code inside the tag and returns a void result. For example, the following markup loops through every item in a collection and produces the item's `Total` property followed by a carriage return:

```
<#foreach(var item in Orders){ #>
    <#= item.Total + Environment.NewLine #>
<# } #>
```

The `<#+ #>` code block is used to define reusable methods, which can be called from inside the T4 template. For example, the following markup defines a method called `TypeName` and returns the full name of the object:

```
<#+  public string Typename(obj){ return obj.GetType().FullName; } #>
```

To use the method, you simply need to call it inside your template file, as illustrated in the following code:

```
<#= Typename(myObj) #>
```

Customizing the generated code for controllers

When adding a new controller class to your ASP.NET MVC project, the **Add New Scaffolded Item** dialog is shown, and you have a choice between three different types of controllers to add:

- **MVC 5 Controller – Empty**
- **MVC 5 Controller with read/write actions**
- **MVC 5 Controller with views, using Entity Framework**

Each of these items generates boilerplate code, which you can customize afterwards. However, let's assume that all our projects' controller classes need a constructor that accepts a parameter. Using the standard items, we would have to manually add the constructor for each controller in our project.

Fortunately, we are able to override the generated output for the controllers, because in essence, they are nothing more than T4 templates.

To customize the output of the **MVC 5 Controller – Empty** item, perform the following steps:

1. Right-click on your ASP.NET MVC project's name inside Visual Studio, and navigate to **Add | New Item**.
2. Navigate to **Visual C# | Web | SideWaffle** and select the **ASP.NET Scaffolding T4 files** item template and click on **Add**:

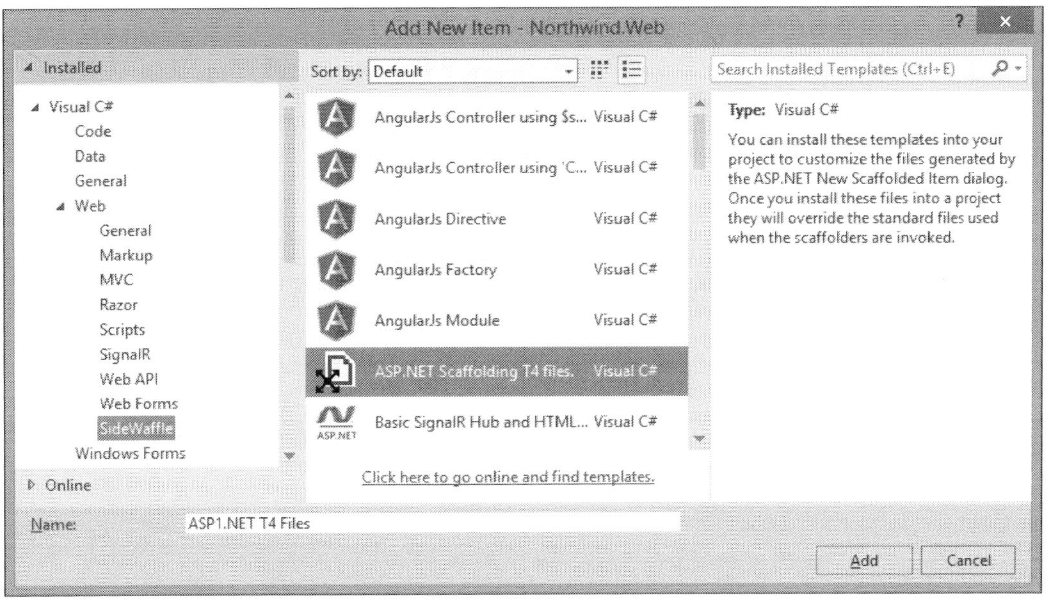

3. The item template will add a folder called `CodeTemplates` inside your project. Inside this folder, it will create 13 subfolders that contain `.t4` files, as shown in the following screenshot:

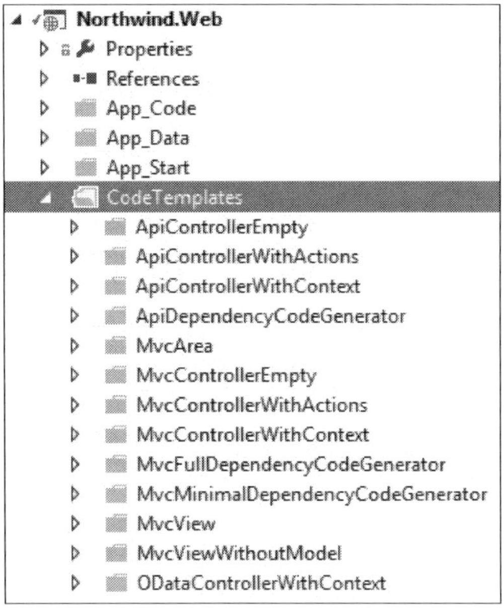

4. Double-click on the `Controller.cs.t4` file inside the `MvcControllerEmpty` folder.
5. The T4 template for the empty MVC 5 controller will open inside Visual Studio. You'll notice that it contains a combination of C# code and T4 markup.
6. Keep the markup in the template as is, but add the following code above the `Index` method:

```
private readonly ApplicationDbContext _context;
private readonly ICurrentUser _currentUser;

public <#= ControllerName #>(ApplicationDbContext context,
ICurrentUser currentUser)
{
    _context = context;
    _currentUser = currentUser;
}
```

7. In the preceding code, we created a constructor for the controller class, and using T4 specifies that the name of the constructor should be the same as the controller name. The `ControllerName` variable is declared at the top of the template file and is automatically passed into the template as follows:

```
<#@ parameter type="System.String" name="ControllerName" #>
```

8. Next, add the following code using declarations just above the namespace:

```
using Northwind.Data.Models;
using Northwind.Infrastructure;
```

9. The `using` statements will ensure that we have the correct references we need when generating a new controller.
10. Save the `Controller.cs.t4` file.
11. Right-click on the `Controllers` folder inside the **Solution Explorer** window and navigate to **Add | Controller**.
12. The standard **Add Scaffold** dialog will be shown; select **MVC 5 Controller - Empty** and click on **Add**.
13. You will be prompted to enter a name for the new controller:

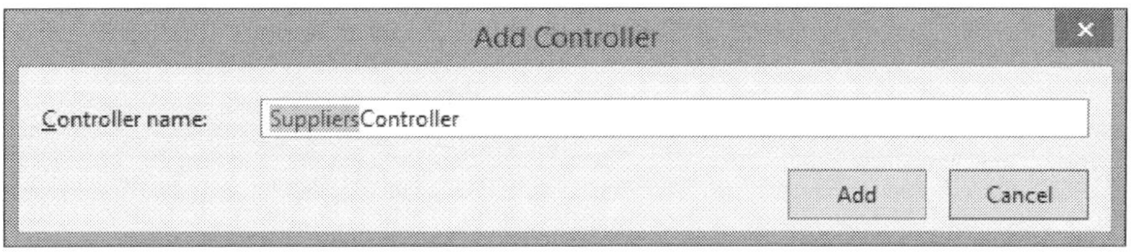

14. Click on **Add** and Visual Studio will scaffold the new controller. The resulting class will now have a constructor that accepts the `ApplicationDbContext` and `ICurrentUser` parameters as follows:

```
using System.Web.Mvc;
using Northwind.Data.Models;
using Northwind.Infrastructure;

namespace Northwind.Web.Controllers
{
    public class SuppliersController : Controller
    {
        private readonly ApplicationDbContext _context;
```

```
            private readonly ICurrentUser _currentUser;

            public SuppliersController(ApplicationDbContext
            context, ICurrentUser currentUser)
            {
                _context = context;
                _currentUser = currentUser;
            }

            //
            // GET: /Suppliers/
            public ActionResult Index()
            {
                return View();
            }
    }
}
```

Customizing the generated code for views

As with controllers, the scaffolding for views can also be customized. In our example project used throughout this book, our views followed a consistent look. Each page has a page header followed by a `breadcrumb` component to indicate to the user which page is currently being viewed.

We always want to follow this design when adding a new page to our site, and one method of enforcing this is to either override the default scaffolder for views or add our own. We'll create a T4 template that will generate a standard, vertical Bootstrap form that already contains a page header and a `breadcrumb` component. To accomplish this, perform the following steps:

1. Open the `MvcView` folder inside the `CodeTemplates` folder.
2. Right-click on the `Create.cs.t4` file and select **Copy**.
3. Right-click on the `MvcView` folder and select **Paste**.
4. The file will be copied as `Create.cs - Copy.t4`; rename it to `VerticalForm-Bootstrap.cs.t4`.
5. Double-click on `VerticalForm-Bootstrap.cs.t4` to open it.
6. Add the following HTML markup before the `@using (Html.BeginForm())` line:

```
<div class="container">
    <div class="page-header">
        <h1><#= ViewDataTypeShortName #> </h1>
    </div>
```

```
<ol class="breadcrumb">
    <li>@Html.ActionLink("Home", "Index", "Home")</li>
    <li class="active"><#= ViewDataTypeShortName #></li>
</ol>

<div class="row clearfix">
    <div class="col-md-12">
```

7. The preceding markup will render a page header and a `breadcrumb` component above the form. The form will reside within a grid column, inside a Bootstrap row's `<div>` element. Note that we use the `ViewDataTypeShortName` variable, which contains the short name of the object used as the model for the view.
8. Next, remove the `<div class="form=horizontal">` line as well as the `<h4>` and `<hr>` elements in the line below `<div>`.
9. Remove all `<div class="form-group">` and `<div class="col-md-10">` elements from the template. Make sure that you also remove all their closing `</div>` tags.
10. Remove the `new { @class = "control-label col-md-2" }` HTML attribute settings from all the `@Html.LabelFor` methods.
11. Lastly, we need to close all the `<div>` elements that were added to the top of the template. Add three closing `</div>` tags after the last `@Html.ActionList` line.

With the template markup in place, we can create a new scaffolded view based on this by completing the following steps:

1. Open a controller class. In this example, we'll use the `SuppliersController.cs` file.
2. Right-click inside the `Index` method and select **Add View...**:

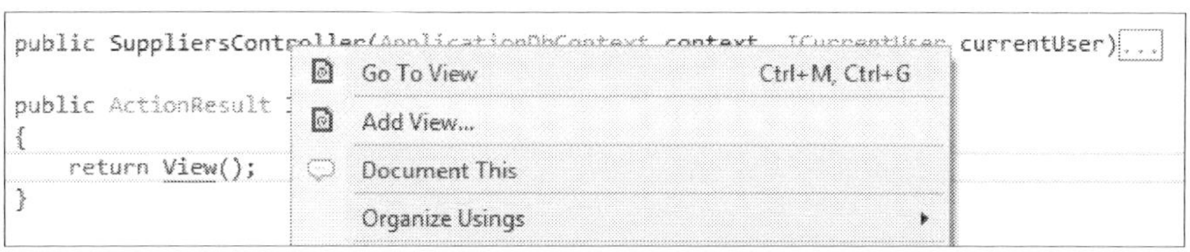

3. This will display the **Add View** dialog.
4. Enter a view name and select the **VerticalForm-Bootstrap** template from the list of templates in the **Template** combobox. Any custom T4 template that you'll create will automatically be listed inside the templates list.
5. Select your model class. In this example, we'll use the **Supplier** model.
6. The **Data context class** field should be automatically selected; if not, select it from the list of data context classes. Click on **Add**:

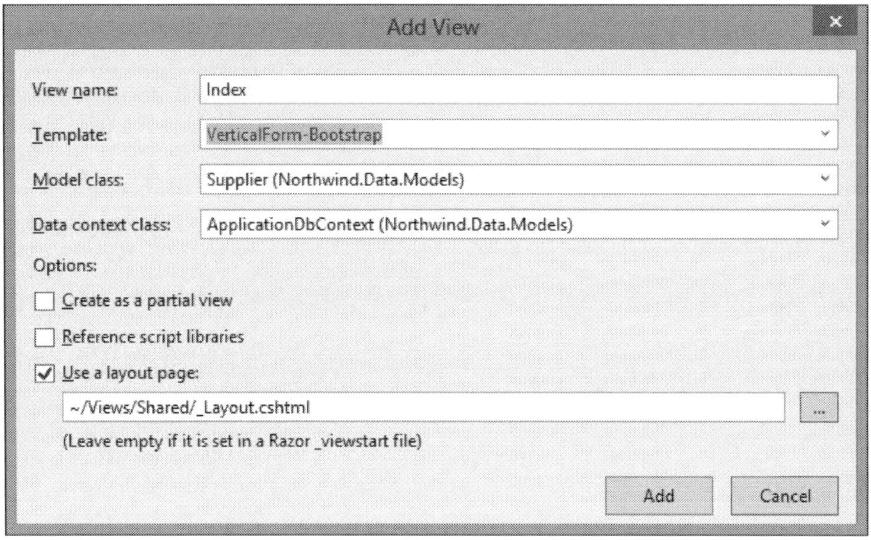

7. Visual Studio will use our custom template to scaffold a view, which will contain all the markup we've added earlier.

8. The result should be a vertical or standard Bootstrap view, as illustrated in the following screenshot:

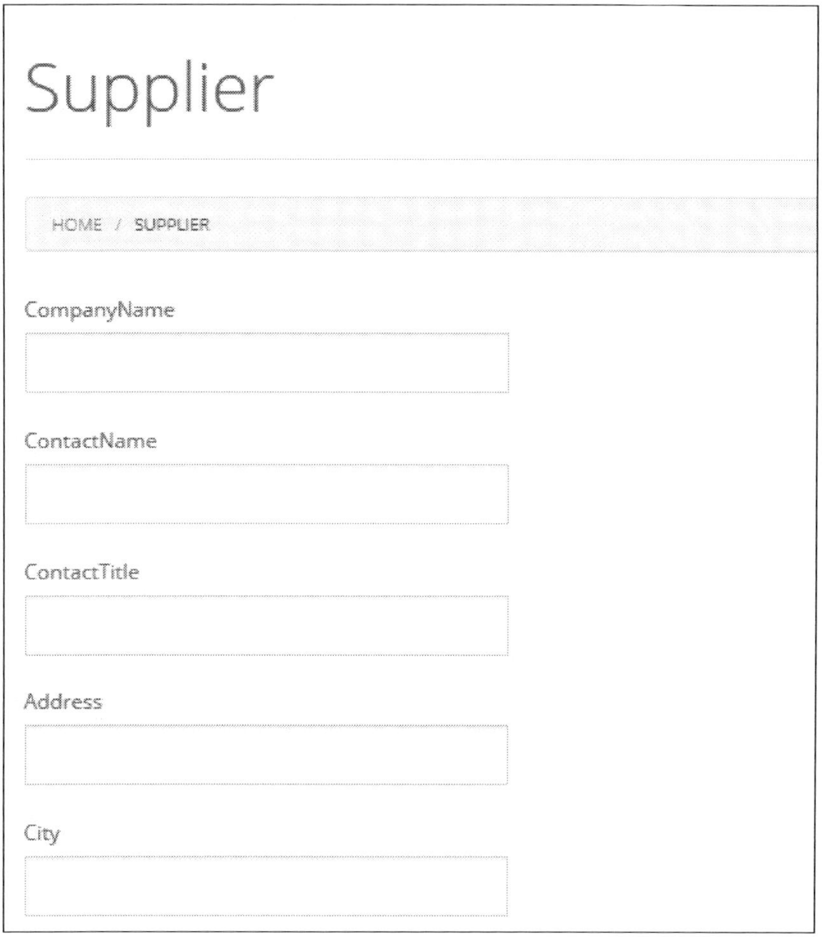

Creating a custom scaffolder extension

If you need more control on how the code for your views or controllers is scaffolded, you need to create a new scaffolding extension for Visual Studio. This extensibility enables developers to add their own scaffolding items to the **Add Scaffold** dialog window, as illustrated in the following screenshot:

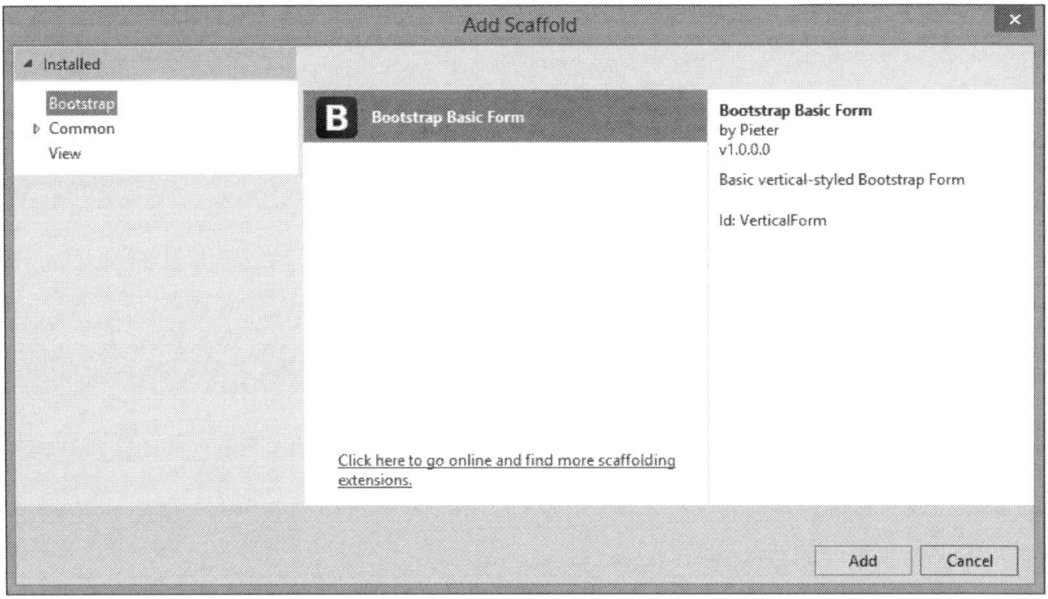

To create such a custom scaffolder, we'll create a new basic scaffolder project. This project template is installed by the SideWaffle extension and adds all the files necessary to create a custom scaffolder.

Perform the following steps to create your own custom scaffolder project:

1. Create a new project inside Visual Studio.
2. Select the **Basic Scaffolder** project template by navigating to **Extensibility | SideWaffle**, as shown in the following screenshot:

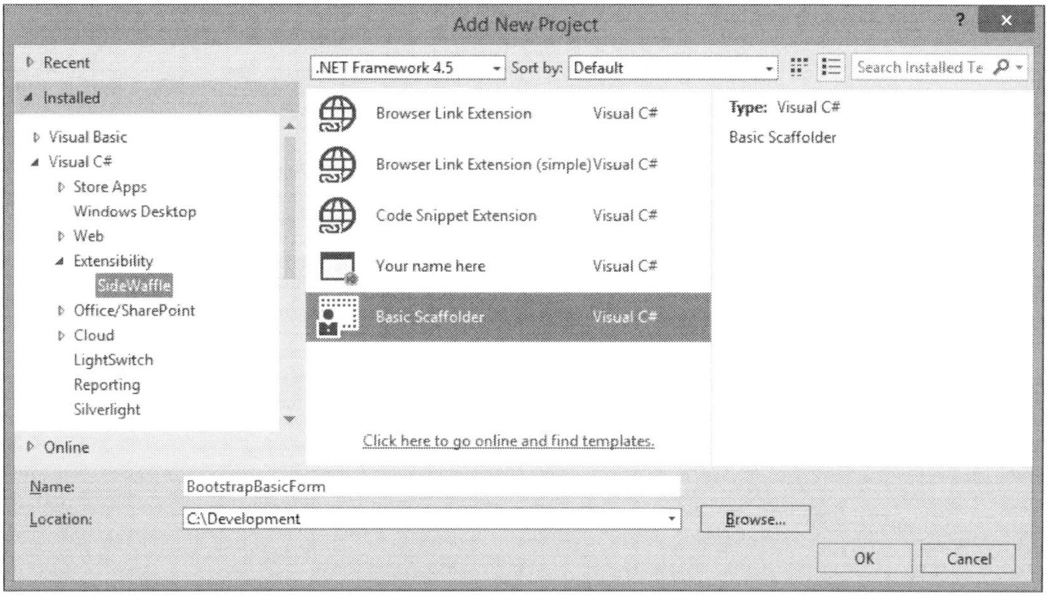

3. The project template will create two new projects: **BootstrapBasicForm** and **BootstrapBasicFormExtension**. One contains the code for the extension and another contains the `.vsixmanifest` file for the project:

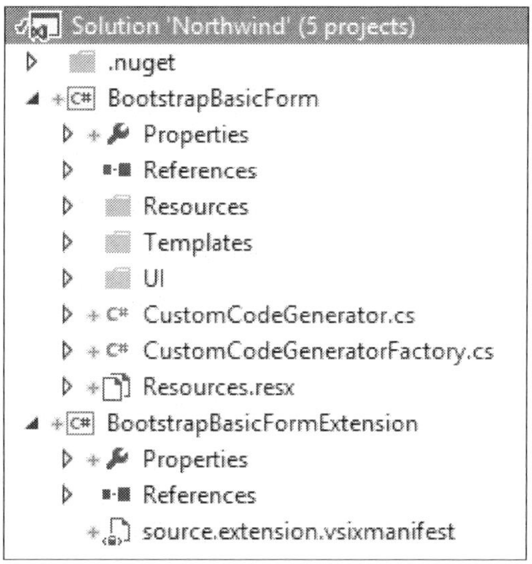

4. Open the **BootstrapBasicFormExtension** project and double-click on the `source.extension.vsixmanifest` file.
5. Visual Studio will open the file in a visual editor in which you can set a range of properties for the extension. For this example, keep everything as is.
6. Open the `CustomCodeGeneratorFactory.cs` file in the **BootstrapBasicForm** project.
7. At the top of this class, a new `CodeGeneratorInformation` object called `_info` is declared. Change it to the following code:

```
private static CodeGeneratorInformation _info = new
CodeGeneratorInformation(
    displayName: "Bootstrap Basic Form",
    description: "Basic vertical-styled Bootstrap Form",
    author: "Pieter",
    version: new Version(1, 0, 0, 0),
    id: typeof(CustomCodeGenerator).Name,
    icon: ToImageSource(Resources._TemplateIconSample),
    gestures: new[] {  "View" },
    categories: new[] { Categories.MvcView, "Bootstrap" });
```

8. The `gestures` parameter indicates when the custom scaffold item will be shown. If the setting is set to `View`, it will only show our custom template when the user adds a new view in Visual Studio.
9. The `categories` parameter is used to set where the template will be shown in the **Add Scaffold** dialog. Categories are shown on the left-hand side of the **Add Scaffold** dialog. You can add your own categories or use the built-in categories.
10. This is all we need to do in the `CustomCodeGeneratorFactory` class. Create a new class called `ServiceProviderExtensions.cs` and add the following code to it:

```
internal static class ServiceProviderExtensions
{
    public static TService GetService<TService>(this
    IServiceProvider provider) where TService : class
    {
        if (provider == null)
        {
            throw new ArgumentNullException("provider");
        }
        return
        (TService)provider.GetService(typeof(TService));
    }
```

```
        public static bool IsServiceAvailable<TService>(this
        IServiceProvider provider) where TService : class
        {
            if (provider == null)
            {
                throw new ArgumentNullException("provider");
            }
            return GetService<TService>(provider) != null;
        }
    }
```

11. Save and close the file, and open the `CustomViewModel.cs` file. This file is located inside the `UI` folder and is used to pass data between UIs, where the user will choose the settings and our code.
12. Add a new property called `ProjectDbContexts` to it. This property will return all valid `DbContext` objects in the project. The code for this property will be as follows:

```
public IEnumerable<ModelType> ProjectDBContexts
{
    get
    {
        ICodeTypeService codeTypeService =
        (ICodeTypeService)Context
            .ServiceProvider.GetService(typeof(ICodeTypeService));

        return codeTypeService
            .GetAllCodeTypes(Context.ActiveProject)
            .Where(codeType =>
             codeType.IsValidDbContextType())
            .Select(codeType => new ModelType(codeType));
    }
}
```

13. Next, add three properties called `Title`, `ControllerName`, and `ViewName` to the class:

```
public string Title { get; set; }
public string ControllerName { get; set; }
public string ViewName { get; set; }
```

14. Lastly, add a `ModelType` property called `SelectedDbContext`:

```
public ModelType SelectedDbContext { get; set; }
```

15. Save and close the file.

16. Double-click on the `SelectModelWindow.xaml` file to open the XAML form designer.
17. This form will be used to prompt the user to select the model and `DbContext` that is to be used to scaffold a view as well as to enter the page title, view, and controller names.
18. The XAML for the form is as follows:

```
<Window x:Class="BasicScaffolder1.UI.SelectModelWindow"
xmlns="http://schemas.microsoft.com/winfx/2006/xaml/presentation"
xmlns:x="http://schemas.microsoft.com/winfx/2006/xaml"
xmlns:mc="http://schemas.openxmlformats.org/markup-
compatibility/2006"
xmlns:d="http://schemas.microsoft.com/expression/blend/2008"
mc:Ignorable="d" Height="233" Width="511" Title="Model Types">
    <Grid>
        <Label Content="Choose a Model Type:"
        HorizontalAlignment="Left"   Margin="36,15,0,0"
        VerticalAlignment="Top"/>
        <ComboBox HorizontalAlignment="Left"
        Margin="169,19,0,0"
        VerticalAlignment="Top"
        ItemsSource="{Binding ModelTypes}"
        DisplayMemberPath="DisplayName"
        SelectedItem="{Binding SelectedModelType,
        Mode=OneWayToSource}"
        Width="311" TabIndex="1"/>
        <Button Content="Add" IsDefault="True"
        HorizontalAlignment="Left" Margin="317,171,0,0"
        VerticalAlignment="Top" Width="75"
        RenderTransformOrigin="-0.187,0.75"
        Click="Button_Click" TabIndex="5"/>

        <Button Content="Cancel" IsCancel="True"
        HorizontalAlignment="Left" VerticalAlignment="Top"
        Width="75" Margin="405,171,0,0" TabIndex="6"/>

        <TextBox x:Name="ControllerNameTextbox"
        HorizontalAlignment="Left" Height="23"
        Margin="169,103,0,0" TextWrapping="Wrap"
        Text="{Binding ControllerName}"
        VerticalAlignment="Top" Width="311" TabIndex="3"/>

        <Label Content="View Name"
        HorizontalAlignment="Left" Margin="36,75,0,0"
        VerticalAlignment="Top"
        RenderTransformOrigin="-0.342,0.269" Width="98"/>
```

```
        <TextBox x:Name="TitleNameTextbox"
        HorizontalAlignment="Left" Height="23"
        Margin="169,131,0,0" TextWrapping="Wrap"
        VerticalAlignment="Top" Width="311" Text="{Binding
        Title}" TabIndex="4"/>

        <Label Content="Controller Name"
        HorizontalAlignment="Left" Margin="36,103,0,0"
        VerticalAlignment="Top"
        RenderTransformOrigin="0.211,-0.154"/>

        <TextBox x:Name="ViewNameTextbox" Text="{Binding
        ViewName}" HorizontalAlignment="Left" Height="23"
        Margin="169,75,0,0" TextWrapping="Wrap"
        VerticalAlignment="Top" Width="311" TabIndex="2"/>

        <Label Content="Title" HorizontalAlignment="Left"
        Margin="36,131,0,0" VerticalAlignment="Top"/>

        <ComboBox HorizontalAlignment="Left"
        Margin="169,46,0,0" VerticalAlignment="Top"
        Width="311" ItemsSource="{Binding
        ProjectDBContexts}" SelectedItem="{Binding
        SelectedDbContext, Mode=OneWayToSource}"
        DisplayMemberPath="DisplayName"/>

        <Label Content="DBContext"
        HorizontalAlignment="Left" Margin="36,46,0,0"
        VerticalAlignment="Top" Width="128"/>

    </Grid>
</Window>
```

19. The preceding XAML markup will bind the form controls to the `CustomViewModel` class. The final design for the form should resemble the following screenshot:

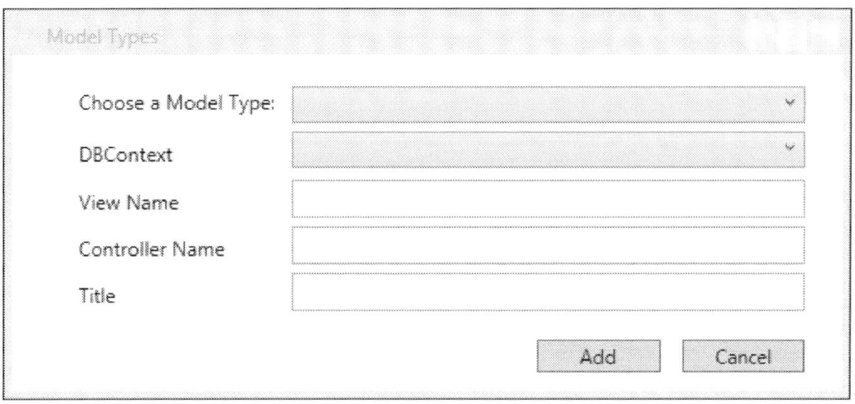

20. Open the `CustomCodeGenerator.cs` file again and replace the `GenerateCode` method with the following code:

```
public override void GenerateCode()
{
    var codeType = _viewModel.SelectedModelType.CodeType;
    var title = _viewModel.Title;
    var controllerName = _viewModel.ControllerName;
    var viewName = _viewModel.ViewName;
    IEntityFrameworkService efService =
      Context.ServiceProvider.GetService<IEntityFrameworkServi
ce>();
    ModelMetadata efMetadata =
      efService.AddRequiredEntity(Context, _viewModel.
SelectedDbContext.TypeName, codeType.FullName);

    var parameters = new Dictionary<string, object>()
    {
        {
            "ModelType", codeType
        },
        {
            "ControllerName", controllerName
        },
        {
            "ViewName", viewName
        },
        {
            "Title", title
        },
        {
            "ModelMetadata",efMetadata
        }
    };

    ProjectItem folder = Context.ActiveProjectItem;
    if (folder.Kind ==
      EnvDTE.Constants.vsProjectItemKindPhysicalFolder)
    {
        var folderName = folder.Name;
        var path = "Views\\" + folderName + "\\" + viewName;
        AddFileFromTemplate(Context.ActiveProject, path,
            "CustomTextTemplate",
```

```
                parameters,
                skipIfExists: false);
        }
    }
```

21. In the preceding code, we added the values captured in the form by the user to a `parameters` collection. We also collected all the metadata about the selected object by using `IEntityFrameworkService`. This service expects a context type name as one of the parameters for its `AddRequiredEntity` method, so we'll pass in the name of the `DbContext` object the user selected on the form.
22. We'll then check whether the user is adding the scaffolded item to a folder, and we'll make a small assumption that the parent folder of the selected folder will be the `Views` folder. We'll then invoke the `AddFileFromTemplate` method.
23. With the UI and view model in place, open the `CustomTextTemplate.cs.t4` file.
24. The top part of the template file specifies the template language, in this case, C# as well as the extension that the template needs to output. Since we're going to scaffold a view, this should be `.cshtml`.
25. We'll also declare all the variables names that will be passed into the template at the top. The following should be added to the top of the template file:

```
<#@ template language="C#" #>
<#@ output extension=".cshtml" #>
<#@ assembly name="System.Core" #>
<#@ assembly name="EnvDTE" #>
<#@ include file="Imports.include.t4" #>
<#@ parameter name="ModelType" type="EnvDTE.CodeType" #>
<#@ parameter name="Title" type="System.String" #>
<#@ parameter name="ControllerName" type="System.String" #>
<#@ parameter name="ViewName" type="System.String" #>
<#@ parameter name="ModelMetadata" type="Microsoft.AspNet.
Scaffolding.Core.Metadata.ModelMetadata"  #>
```

26. The rest of the T4 markup for the template is as follows:

```
@model <#= ModelType.Namespace.FullName #>.<#= ModelType.Name #>


@{
    ViewBag.Title = "<#= Title #>";
```

```
    Layout = "~/Views/Shared/_Layout.cshtml";
}

<div class="container">
    <div class="page-header">
        <h1><#= Title #> </h1>
    </div>

    <ol class="breadcrumb">
        <li>@Html.ActionLink("Home", "Index", "Home")</li>
        <li class="active"><#= Title #></li>
    </ol>

    <div class="row clearfix">
        <div class="col-md-12">
            @using (Html.BeginForm("<#= ViewName #>", "<#=
            ControllerName #>", FormMethod.Post, new { role
            = "form" }))
            {
                @Html.AntiForgeryToken()
                @Html.ValidationSummary(true)

    <#
      foreach (PropertyMetadata property in
      ModelMetadata.Properties)
        {
          #>
            <div class="form-group">
              @Html.LabelFor(model => model.<#=
              property.PropertyName #>)
            </div>
          <#
        }
    #>
    </div>
  </div>
```

27. At this point, you are ready to test the custom scaffold item by running your project. An experimental instance of Visual Studio will start; open an existing ASP.NET MVC project and right-click on a subfolder inside the `Views` folder and navigate to **Add | View...**. You should see your custom scaffold item in the Bootstrap category, and when you double-click on it, the custom form we created should be shown.

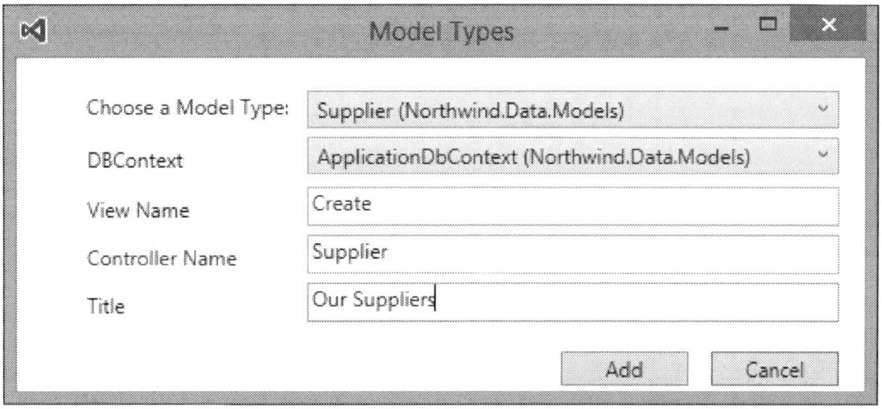

By clicking on **Add**, the new view will be created inside the selected folder and the variables inside the template will be populated with the values entered on the form.

Summary

In this chapter, we explored the possibilities of how to customize the built-in ASP.NET MVC scaffolding templates, how to add your own ones, and even how to build your own advanced scaffolder with its own custom UI.

In the next chapter, we'll further investigate how to convert a standard HTML web template into a reusable ASP.NET MVC Visual Studio project.

7
Converting a Bootstrap HTML Template into a Usable ASP.NET MVC Project

One of the major benefits of using Bootstrap is the wide variety of resources available on the Internet. The web development community embraced Bootstrap, and you'll find tons of valuable templates, snippets, and advice on using Bootstrap.

By combining a predesigned Bootstrap template and ASP.NET MVC, you can save a lot of time without having to worry about site layout or design.

In this chapter, we will cover the following topics:

- Why we use prebuilt HTML templates and how they will save time
- Building the master layout
- Adding specific page views
- Including charts in your views

Working with prebuilt HTML templates

It is a well-known fact that most developers are not necessarily good designers. We prefer to work on the backend, building great-performing and intelligent software, and sometimes, we tend to think of the user interface as an afterthought.

By using a predesigned HTML Bootstrap template, we can give our users an intuitive and well-designed user interface that was designed by a professional designer. If the design was based on Bootstrap, the developer is already familiar with most of the CSS class names, components, and plugins, and does not have to relearn anything.

The Web offers an assortment of free and premium Bootstrap templates. ThemeForest (`www.themeforest.net`) provides a mind-boggling array of different premium site styles and designs.

For our example in this chapter, we'll use the free SB Admin 2 template designed by Start Bootstrap (`www.startbootstrap.com`). The SB Admin 2 template is an admin theme that uses Bootstrap 3 and is ideal for a backend administration or more complex style web application. The theme looks like the following screenshot:

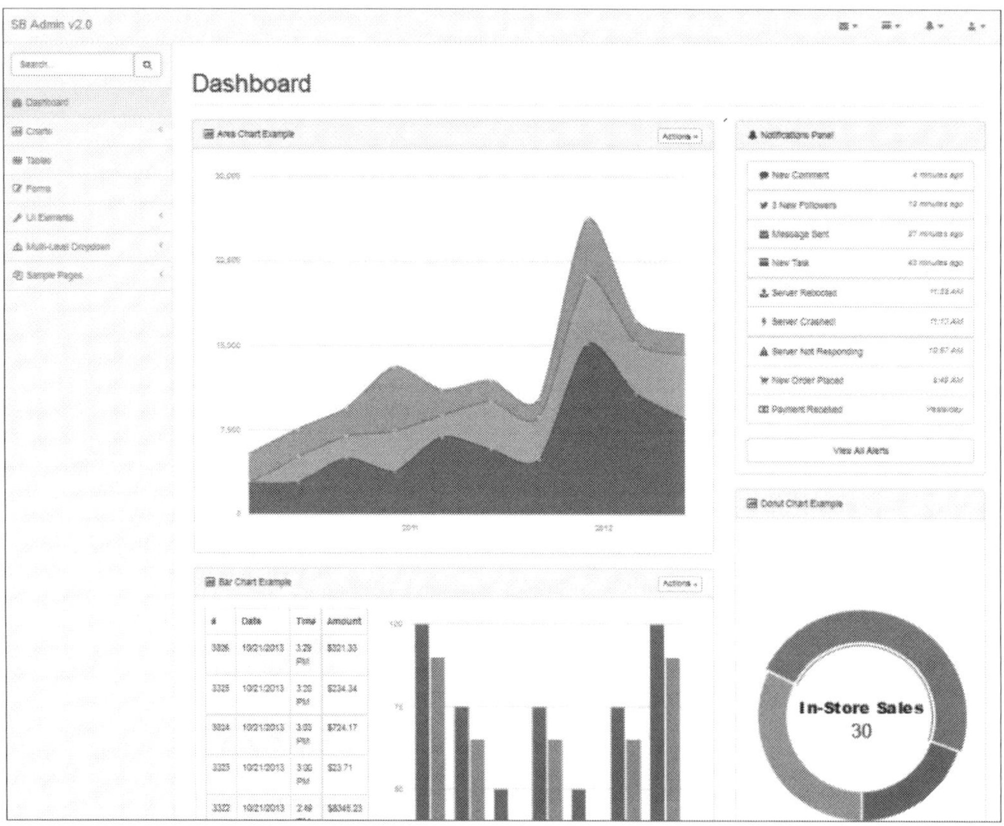

Before we can build an ASP.NET MVC site with the template, we need to download the source files by completing the following steps:

1. Navigate to `http://startbootstrap.com/sb-admin-v2` and click on the **Download** button to download a zip archive that contains all the necessary HTML, CSS, and JavaScript files.
2. Extract the files to a folder on your local hard drive; you'll notice that the archive contains the familiar Bootstrap folders:
   - `css`
   - `font-awesome`
   - `fonts`
   - `js`
3. The archive also contains a number of HTML files that illustrate various page and component layouts of the template, as shown in the following screenshot:

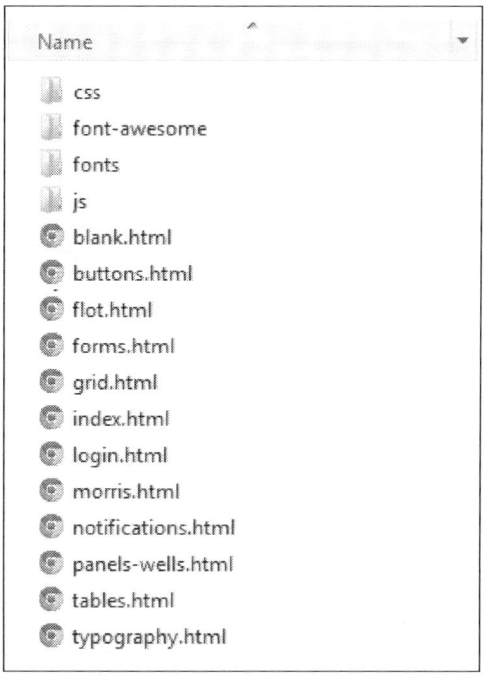

Creating the ASP.NET MVC project

To create a new ASP.NET MVC project, perform the following steps:

1. In Visual Studio, create a new **ASP.NET Web Application** project, as shown in the following screenshot:

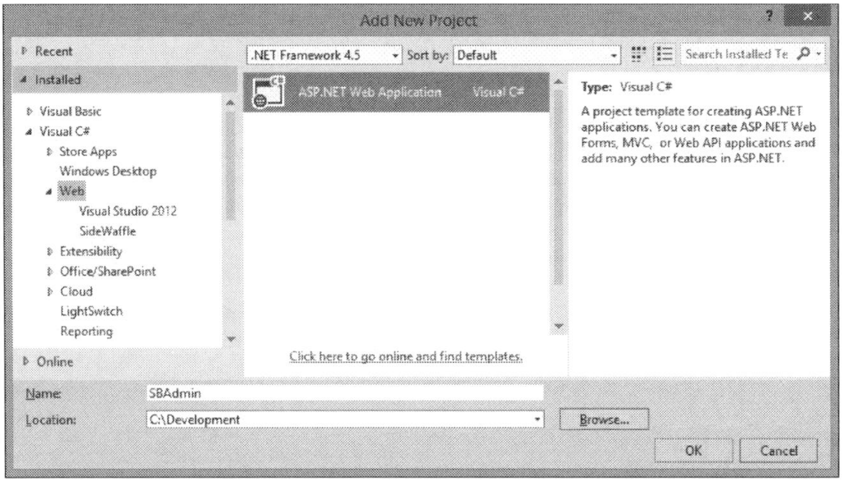

2. In the **New ASP.NET Project** dialog, select the **Empty** template, check the **MVC** checkbox, and click on the **OK** button.

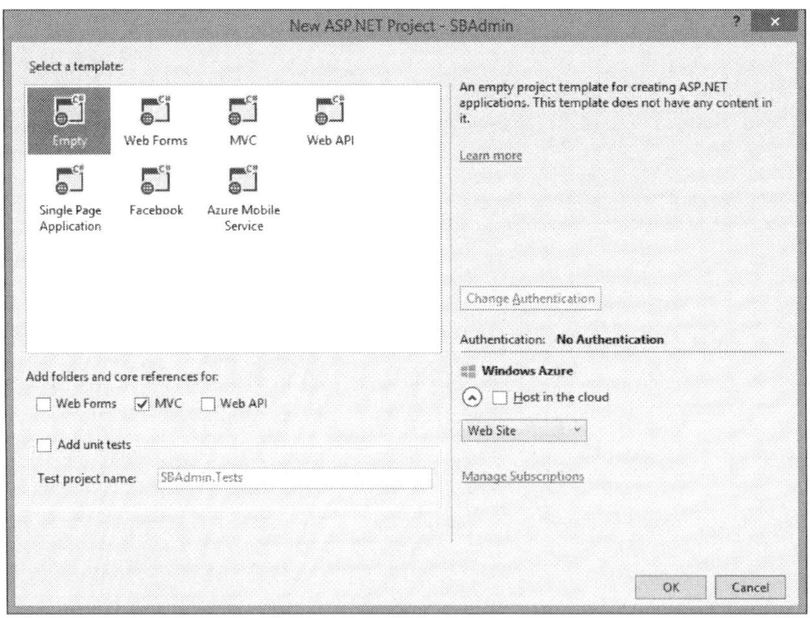

3. Visual Studio will create a default empty MVC project. Right-click on the project name and navigate to **Add** | **New Folder**. Create the following four folders:
    - `css`
    - `font-awesome`
    - `fonts`
    - `js`
4. Add the following `.css` files from the SB Admin source `css` folder to the `css` folder inside your project:
    - `bootstrap.css`
    - `sb-admin.css`
5. Add the `font-awesome.css` file inside the SB Admin source's `font-awesome\css` folder to the `css` folder in your project.
6. Add all the files inside the SB Admin source's `fonts` and `font-awesome\fonts` folder to the `fonts` folder inside your project.
7. Add the following files from the SB Admin source's `js` folder to the `js` folder in your project:
    - `bootstrap.js`
    - `sb-admin.js`

Creating the master layout

We've added the CSS, JavaScript, and Font files needed to create the master layout file for our project. Next, we need to create a home controller as well as a master layout file. To do this, complete the following steps:

1. Right-click on the `Controllers` folder and navigate to **Add** | **Controller...**.
2. Select **MVC 5 Controller - Empty** from the **Add Scaffold** dialog window and click on **Add**.

3. Enter `HomeController` in the **Controller name** textbox in the **Add Controller** dialog window, and click on **Add**.

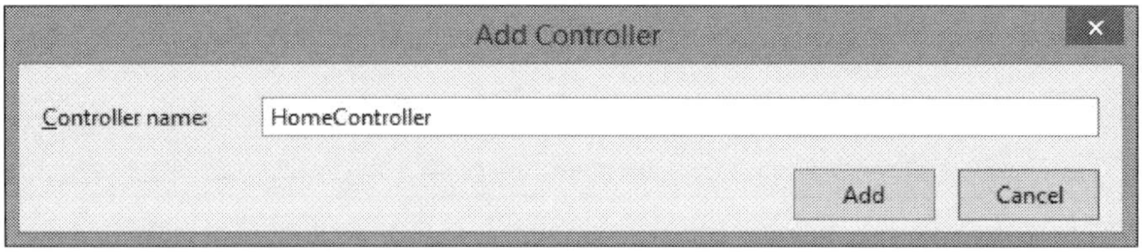

4. Next, right-click on the `Views` folder in your project and navigate to **Add** | **New Folder**. Name the folder `Shared`.
5. Right-click on the newly-created `Shared` folder and navigate to **Add** | **MVC 5 Layout Page (Razor)**.
6. In the **Specify Name for Item** dialog, type `_Layout` in the **Item name** textbox and click on **OK**.

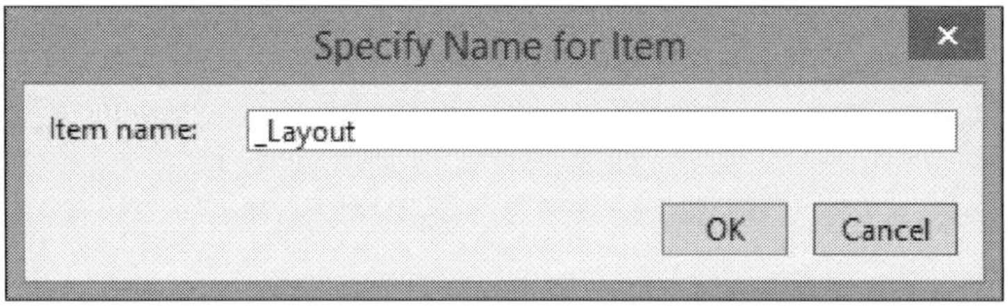

7. Open the `blank.html` file in the SB Admin source files and copy its contents to the `_Layout.cshtml` file.
8. Change the `<head>` tag to the following code:

```
<head>
    <meta charset="utf-8">
    <meta name="viewport" content="width=device-width,
    initial-scale=1.0">
    <title>Start Bootstrap - SB Admin Version 2.0 ::
    @ViewBag.Title</title>
    <link href="@Url.Content("~/css/bootstrap.css")"
    rel="stylesheet">
    <link href="@Url.Content("~/css/font-awesome.css")"
    rel="stylesheet">
    <link href="@Url.Content("~/css/sb-admin.css")"
    rel="stylesheet">
</head>
```

9. In the preceding markup, we used the `Url.Content` helper to map a virtual path to the `.css` files in our project.
10. Add the following code just above the closing `</body>` tag:

```
<script src="//ajax.googleapis.com/ajax/libs/jquery/1.11.1/jquery.
min.js"></script>
<script src="@Url.Content("~/js/bootstrap.js")"></script>
<script src="@Url.Content("~/js/sb-admin.js")"></script>
@RenderSection("scripts", false)
```

11. In the preceding code, we added a reference to the jQuery library that is hosted on a Google **Content Delivery Network** (**CDN**). We also used the `Url.Content` helper again to map a virtual path to the required JavaScript files and used the `@RenderSection` helper to specify a section called `scripts`.
12. Next, you'll notice that the page is divided into three distinguishable elements:
    - A `<div>` element whose ID is set to `wrapper`
    - A `<nav>` element
    - A `<div>` element with an ID of `page-wrapper`
13. Leave the `<nav>` and `<div id="wrapper">` elements as is, and replace all markup inside the `<div id="page-wrapper">` element with the `@RenderBody()` method.
14. The master layout is now complete; next, we'll need to add a view for the `Index` action on the home controller.

Adding a view for the home controller

We need to create a view for the home controller's `Index` action in order to test our template. Complete the following steps to accomplish this:

1. Open the `HomeController.cs` file, right-click inside the `Index` method, and select `Add View...` from the context-menu.
2. In the **Add View** dialog, set the **View name** textbox to `Index` and the **Template** combobox to **Empty (without model)**.

3. Tick the **Use a layout page** checkbox, and select the `_Layout.cshtml` file we created earlier as the layout page. Click on **Add**.

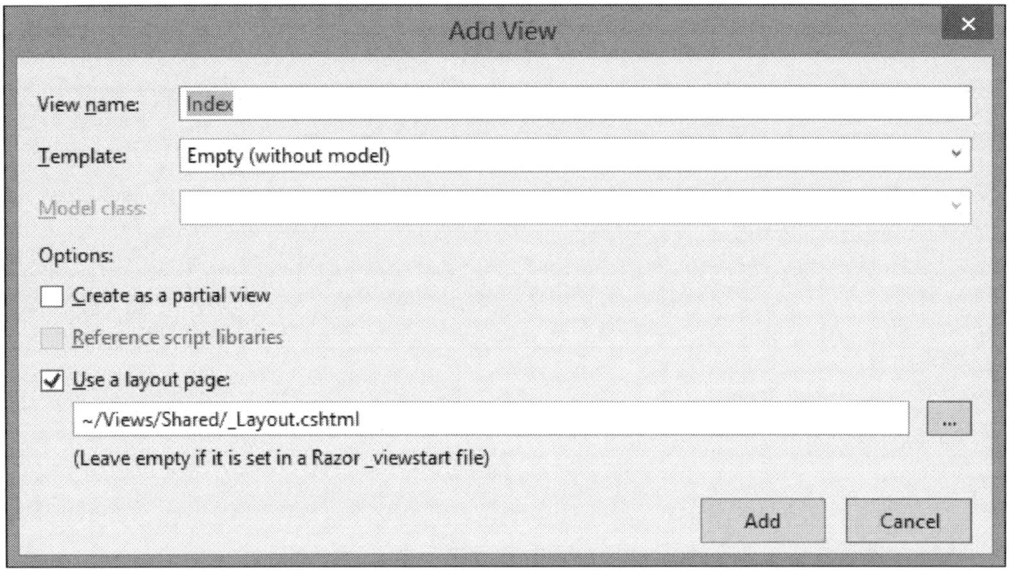

4. An `Index.cshtml` file will be created inside the `Views\Home` folder.
5. Add the following markup to the view:

```
@{
    ViewBag.Title = "Index";
    Layout = "~/Views/Shared/_Layout.cshtml";
}
<div class="row">
    <div class="col-lg-12">
        <h1 class="page-header">Blank</h1>
    </div>
</div>
```

6. Run your project, and you should see the home view and layout in your browser. Note that the left-hand side menu will be expanded to display all items, as shown in the following screenshot:

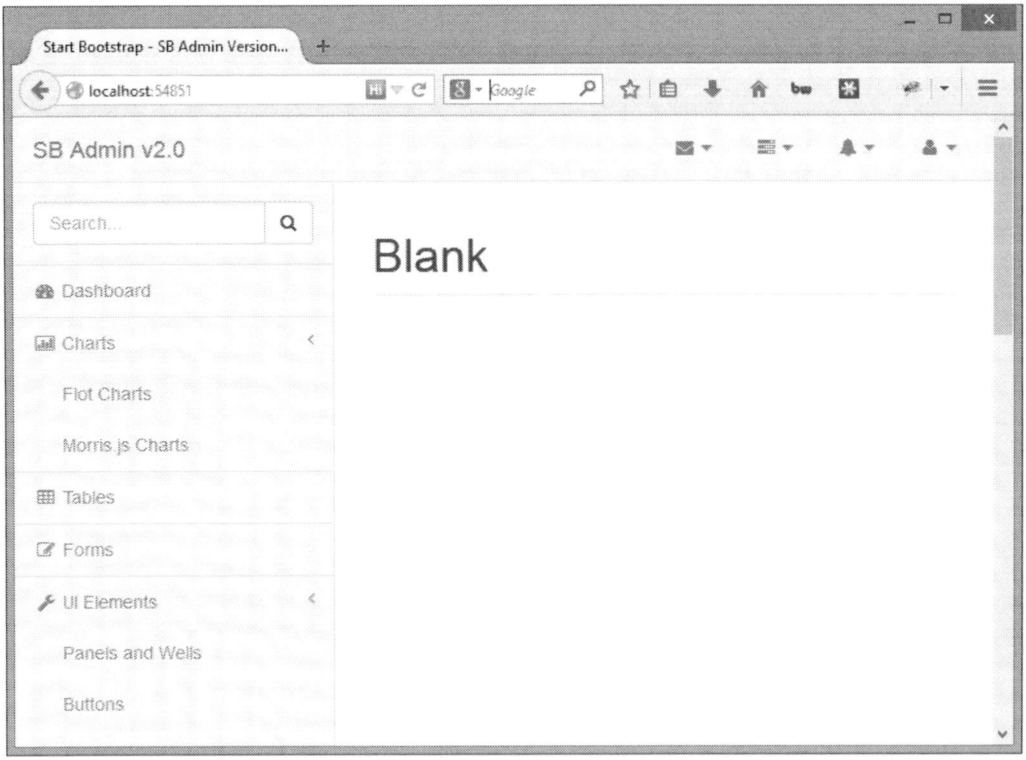

Adding the menu plugin library

Currently, the left-hand side menu displays all the items. We need the menu to expand only when the user clicks on the appropriate menu item. To enable this, we'll need to add a reference to the metisMenu jQuery plugin to our master layout page. For this, perform the following steps:

1. Add a subfolder called `plugins` to the `js` folder in your project.
2. Add a new folder inside the `plugins` folder called `metisMenu`.
3. Add the `jquery.metisMenu.js` file inside the SB Admin source files' `js\plugins\metisMenu` folder to the `plugins\metisMenu` folder inside your project.
4. Next, open the `_Layout.cshtml` file inside the `Views\Shared` folder.

5. Add a reference to the metisMenu plugin by adding the following line just above the `</body>` closing element:

```
<script src="@Url.Content("~/js/plugins/metisMenu/jquery.
metisMenu.js")"></script>
```

6. When running your project, the left-hand side menu should now display correctly.

Adding different page views

The SB Admin template comes with a variety of different page styles, which can be used to build our own views. We'll create a custom view that displays two panels, one with a simple Bootstrap form and another one that displays an image, by completing the following steps:

1. Add a new empty MVC 5 controller called `FormsController` to your project.
2. Add a new empty view for the `Index` method of the controller and select the layout page we've created earlier as its layout page.
3. Open the `Index.cshtml` file inside the `Views\Forms` folder.
4. Add the following markup to the view:

```
@{
    ViewBag.Title = "Index";
    Layout = "~/Views/Shared/_Layout.cshtml";
}

<div class="row">
    <div class="col-lg-12">
        <h1 class="page-header">Forms</h1>
    </div>
</div>
<div class="row">
    <div class="col-lg-6">
        <div class="panel panel-primary">
            <div class="panel-heading">
                Firs Panel with simple form
            </div>
            <div class="panel-body">
                <div class="row">
                    <div class="col-lg-6">
                        <form role="form">
```

```
                            <div class="form-group">
                                <label>Full name</label>
                                <input class="form-control"
placeholder="Your full name">
                            </div>
                            <div class="form-group">
                                <label>Bio</label>
                                <textarea class="form-control"
rows="3"></textarea>
                            </div>

                            <div class="form-group">
                                <label>Subject</label>
                                <label class="checkbox-inline">
                                    <input type="checkbox">Math
                                </label>
                                <label class="checkbox-inline">
                                    <input type="checkbox">Science
                                </label>
                                <label class="checkbox-inline">
                                    <input type="checkbox">History
                                </label>
                            </div>
                            <button type="submit" class="btn btn-
primary">Save</button>
                        </form>
                    </div>
                </div>
            </div>
        </div>
    </div>
    <div class="col-lg-6">
        <div class="panel panel-danger">
            <div class="panel-heading">
                Second Panel
            </div>
            <div class="panel-body">
                <div class="row">
                    <div class="col-lg-6">
                        <p>This is a second panel on the page</p>
                        <img src="http://placehold.it/350x150"
alt="placeholder" />
```

```
                    </div>
                </div>
            </div>
        </div>
    </div>
</div>
```

5. The preceding code will render two panels, one blue and one red, as illustrated in the following screenshot:

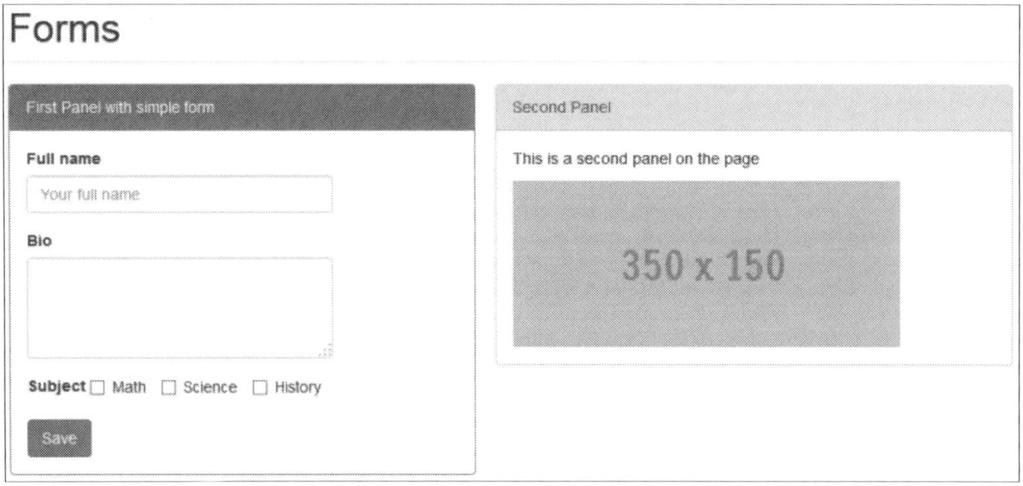

Finally, we need to change the left-hand side navigation menu to include a link to the view we just added. To accomplish this, complete the following steps:

1. Open the `_Layout.cshtml` file inside the `Views\Shared` folder.
2. Find the following line of code inside the file:

```
<a href="tables.html"><i class="fa fa-table fa-fw"></i> Tables</a>
```

3. Replace the preceding line with the following:

```
<a href="@Url.Action("Index","Forms")"><i class="fa fa-table
fa-fw"></i> Form</a>
```

4. We used the `@Url.Action` helper to navigate the user to the `Index` action of the forms' controller. When the user clicks on the **Forms** menu item, they will be shown the form view we created earlier.

Adding charts to your views

In the SB Admin template, the **Dashboard** page contains a variety of attractive charts and graphs that you can use to display data in an interactive way to your users. We'll add the **Dashboard** page and its functionality that is included in the SB Admin template to our project by completing the following steps:

1. Create a new folder called `morris` inside the `js\plugins` folder.
2. Add the following two files from the SB Admin source files to the folder:
    - `raphael-2.1.0.min.js`
    - `morris.js`
3. Add the `dashboard-demo.js` file to the `js` folder.
4. Add the `morris-0.4.3.min.css` file to your project's `css` folder.
5. Next, open the `_Layout.cshtml` file and add the following code to the `<head>` element:

    ```
    @RenderSection("styles",false)
    ```

6. By adding the preceding line, we can inject additional CSS styles into the layout page per view.
7. Open the `Index.cshtml` file inside the `Views\Home` folder.
8. Add the following code to the top of the file, just below the layout declaration:

    ```
    @section styles{
        <link href="@Url.Content("~/css//morris-0.4.3.min.css")"
    rel="stylesheet">
    }
    ```

9. The preceding code will inject the styles for the `morris` chart component into our view.
10. Add the following markup to the view:

    ```
    <div class="row">
        <div class="col-lg-12">
            <h1 class="page-header">Dashboard</h1>
        </div>
    </div>
    <div class="row">
        <div class="col-lg-12">
            <div class="panel panel-default">
    ```

```
                <div class="panel-heading">
                    <i class="fa fa-bar-chart-o fa-fw"></i> Area Chart
Example
                    <div class="pull-right">
                        <div class="btn-group">
                            <button type="button" class="btn btn-
default btn-xs dropdown-toggle" data-toggle="dropdown">
                                Actions
                                <span class="caret"></span>
                            </button>
                            <ul class="dropdown-menu pull-right"
                            role="menu">
                                <li>
                                    <a href="#">Action</a>
                                </li>
                                <li>
                                    <a href="#">Another action</a>
                                </li>
                                <li>
                                    <a href="#">Something else
                                    here</a>
                                </li>
                                <li class="divider"></li>
                                <li>
                                    <a href="#">Separated link</a>
                                </li>
                            </ul>
                        </div>
                    </div>
                </div>
                <div class="panel-body">
                    <div id="morris-area-chart"></div>
                </div>
            </div>
        </div>
    </div>
```

11. Next, add the following section declaration, which will inject the necessary JavaScript files for the charting components into the view, to the bottom of the file:

```
@section scripts{
    <script src="@Url.Content("~/js/plugins/morris/raphael-
2.1.0.min.js")"></script>
```

```
    <script src="@Url.Content("~/js/plugins/morris/morris.js")"></
script>
    <script src="@Url.Content("~/js/dashboard-demo.js")"></script>
}
```

12. Finally, open the `_Layout.cshtml` file and find the following line:

```
<a href="index.html"><i class="fa fa-dashboard fa-fw"></i>
Dashboard</a>
```

13. Change the identified line to the following line:

```
<a href="@Url.Action("Index","Home")"><i class="fa fa-dashboard
fa-fw"></i> Dashboard</a>
```

14. Save and close all files and run your project.
15. You should see a chart rendered, similar to the following screenshot, when you navigate to the **Dashboard** page.

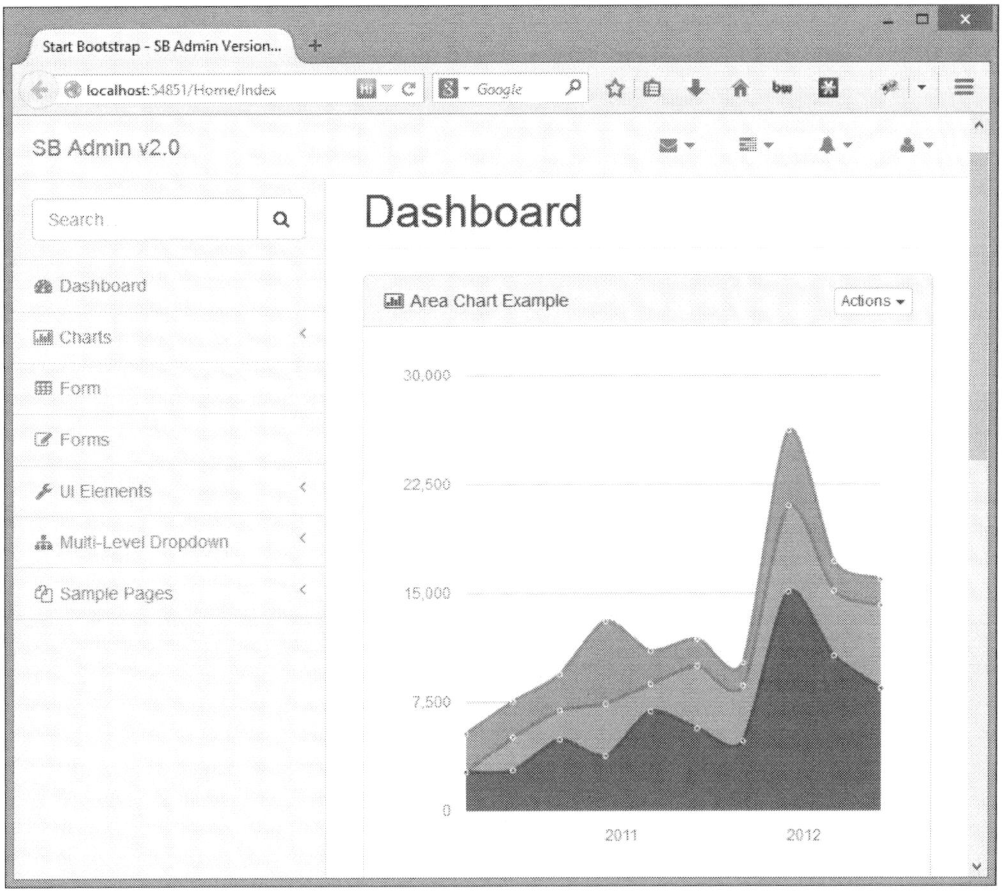

Summary

In this chapter, you've learned how to convert a predesigned HTML template into a usable ASP.NET MVC project. The techniques shown in this chapter can be applied to virtually any HTML template, allowing you to build professionally-designed web applications without having to design the layout yourself.

In the next chapter, we'll explore how to include and use the jQuery DataTables plugin in your own ASP.NET MVC projects.

8

Using the jQuery DataTables Plugin with Bootstrap

The jQuery DataTables plugin allows developers to add innovative interaction controls to any HTML table.

The jQuery DataTables plugin supports a multitude of options and a rich range of extensions. ASP.NET MVC developers are also able to include this plugin in their own projects. The purpose of this chapter is not only to show you how to use the DataTables plugin, but also to illustrate how you can use almost any open source JavaScript and CSS plugin or framework with ASP.NET MVC.

In this chapter, we will cover the following topics:

- An overview of jQuery DataTables
- Including the jQuery DataTables plugin in your ASP.NET MVC project
- Loading and displaying data with jQuery DataTables and ASP.NET MVC
- Using some of the extensions

jQuery DataTables

DataTables is a free, open source plugin for the jQuery JavaScript library that is designed and created by a company called SpryMedia Ltd. This plugin makes adding features such as ordering, filtering, pagination, and searching to any standard HTML table incredibly easy to implement.

It also offers various extensions that enable Excel-like features, inline editing, and fixed columns to name a few. The DataTables website offers well-documented examples, a blog, and a forum, which you can find at `www.datatables.net`.

The jQuery DataTables plugin can be added to your ASP.NET MVC project in one of the two ways, the DataTables NuGet package or **Content Delivery Network** (**CDN**).

Adding DataTables to your ASP.NET MVC project

To add the basic functionality for the DataTables plugin, the following two files are required:

- The first is `jquery.dataTables.css` and it contains the default CSS styling for the tables
- The second is `jquery.dataTables.js` and it contains the JavaScript logic for rendering the DataTables plugin and adding the necessary functionality

Both these files are available at the DataTables CDN at the following links:

- `//cdn.datatables.net/1.10.0/css/jquery.dataTables.css`
- `//cdn.datatables.net/1.10.0/js/jquery.dataTables.js`

Using the DataTables NuGet package

You can also add all the required CSS and JavaScript files needed for jQuery DataTables as well as all the CSS and JavaScript files for the extensions using NuGet. Complete the following steps to add jQuery DataTables when using NuGet:

1. In Visual Studio, open the **Package Manager Console** window by navigating to **Tools** | **Library Package Manager** | **Package Manager Console**.
2. Inside the **Package Manager Console** window, type the following command:
   ```
   Install-Package jquery.datatables
   ```
3. The NuGet package will add a `DataTables-1.10.0` folder inside the `Content` folder, which contains the `css`, `images`, and `swf` files required for the DataTables plugin.
4. It will also add a `DataTables-1.10.0` folder to the `Scripts` folder in your project. This folder will contain JavaScript files for the DataTables plugin as well as JavaScript files for all the extensions.

Using the CDN

You can either save the files from the aforementioned locations or add them to your project or rather add a reference to the files hosted on the CDN, which is the preferred approach. This will help in increasing your site's performance. To reference it from the CDN, complete the following steps:

1. In Visual Studio, open this book's accompanying sample project and open the `_Layout.cshtml` file located inside the `Views\Shared` folder.
2. Inside the `<head>` element of the `_Layout.cshtml` file, add a reference to the jQuery DataTables style sheet by inserting the following line of markup:

```
<link rel="stylesheet" type="text/css" href="//cdn.datatables.
net/1.10.0/css/jquery.dataTables.css">
```

3. Open the view in which you'll need the DataTables functionality and add a reference to the JavaScript library by adding the following code to the bottom of the view:

```
@section scripts{
    <script type="text/javascript" language="javascript" src="//
cdn.datatables.net/1.10.0/js/jquery.dataTables.min.js"></script>
}
```

Adding Bootstrap styling to DataTables

The steps mentioned in the preceding section will add the minimum required files to the view and layout file in order to generate the basic styling and functionality for jQuery DataTables. However, the default DataTables CSS styles can look somewhat out of place inside a Bootstrap website.

Luckily, the team behind the DataTables project created a Bootstrap-specific CSS style and JavaScript library to match the look and feel of your site. Both these files are also available on the DataTables CDN:

- `//cdn.datatables.net/plug-ins/be7019ee387/integration/bootstrap/3/dataTables.bootstrap.css`
- `//cdn.datatables.net/plug-ins/be7019ee387/integration/bootstrap/3/dataTables.bootstrap.js`

These two files are added in the same way as the normal DataTables CSS and JavaScript files. Bear in mind that when including the Bootstrap-specific DataTables JavaScript file in your view, you need to include a reference to both the default DataTables JavaScript files as well as the Bootstrap-specific file, as illustrated in the following markup:

```
<script type="text/javascript" language="javascript" src="//cdn.
datatables.net/1.10.0/js/jquery.dataTables.min.js"></script>
<script type="text/javascript" language="javascript" src="//cdn.
datatables.net/plug-ins/be7019ee387/integration/bootstrap/3/
dataTables.bootstrap.js"></script>
```

Loading and displaying data in jQuery DataTables

In order to implement the jQuery DataTables plugin, we first need to create a new view that will list data inside an HTML table. For this example, we'll create a view that lists customers from the Northwind Traders database. For this, complete the following steps:

1. In Visual Studio, add a new controller class called `CustomersController.cs`.
2. We've implemented a dependency injection in our project, so we'll add a constructor to the class that will automatically set the reference to the database context with the following code:

   ```
   public CustomersController(ApplicationDbContext context)
   {
       _context = context;
   }
   ```

3. The `_context` object is a local field declared inside the class as follows:

   ```
   private readonly ApplicationDbContext _context;
   ```

4. Add a new method called `Index` to the controller. This method returns an `ActionResult` object to the controller. Add the following code to it that will pass a list of customer objects to the view:

   ```
   public ActionResult Index()
   {
       var model = _context.Customers;
       return View(model);
   }
   ```

5. Right-click inside the `Index` method and select **Add View...** from the context-menu.
6. In the **Add View** dialog window, change the **Template** combobox value to **List** and select the **Customer** object as **Model class**. Click on **Add**, as shown in the following screenshot:

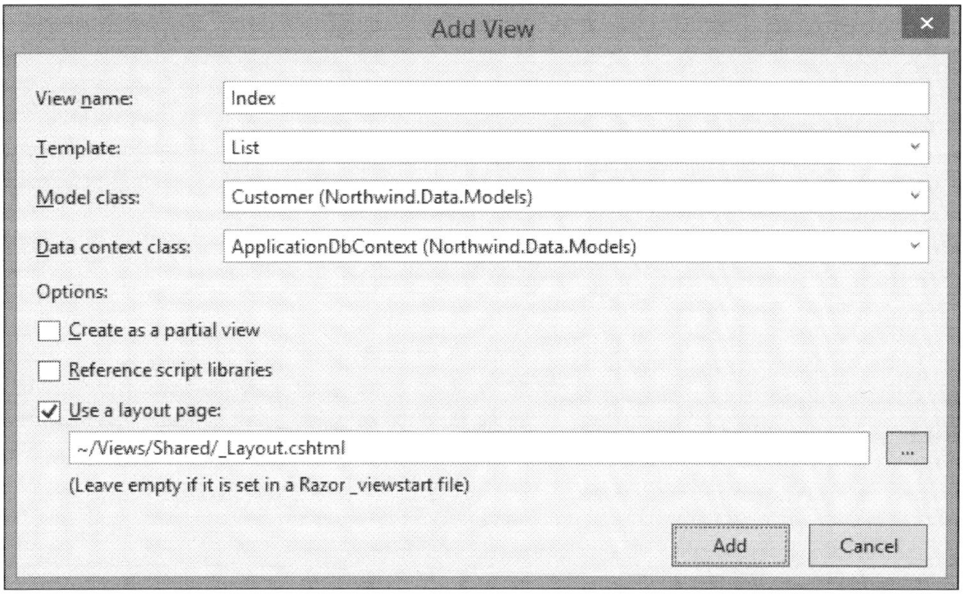

7. Visual Studio will scaffold the default list view for the `Customer` object. We won't need all the columns for the view, and we'll add a page header and the `breadcrumb` component to the top of the page. The final markup for the view should look like the following code:

```
@model IEnumerable<Northwind.Data.Models.Customer>

@{
    ViewBag.Title = "Customers";
    Layout = "~/Views/Shared/_Layout.cshtml";
}
<div class="container">
    <div class="page-header">
```

```
        <h1>Customers <small>Our Customers</small></h1>
    </div>

    <ol class="breadcrumb">
        <li>@Html.ActionLink("Home", "Index", "Home")</li>
        <li class="active">Customers</li>
    </ol>
    <table class="table table-striped table-hover">
        <thead>
            <tr>
                <th>
                    @Html.DisplayNameFor(model => model.
                    CustomerCode)
                </th>
                <th>
                    @Html.DisplayNameFor(model => model.
                    CompanyName)
                </th>
                <th>
                    @Html.DisplayNameFor(model => model.
                    ContactName)
                </th>
                <th>
                    @Html.DisplayNameFor(model => model.City)
                </th>
                <th>
                    @Html.DisplayNameFor(model => model.Country)
                </th>
                <th>
                    @Html.DisplayNameFor(model => model.Phone)
                </th>
            </tr>
        </thead>
        <tbody>
            @foreach (var item in Model)
            {
                <tr>
                    <td>
                        @Html.ActionLink(item.CustomerCode,
                        "Edit", new { id = item.CustomerId })
                    </td>
                    <td>
                        @Html.DisplayFor(modelItem => item.
                        CompanyName)
                    </td>
                    <td>
                        @Html.DisplayFor(modelItem => item.
                        ContactName)
                    </td>
                    <td>.
```

```
                        @Html.DisplayFor(modelItem => item.City)
                    </td>
                    <td>
                        @Html.DisplayFor(modelItem => item.
                        Country)
                    </td>
                    <td>
                        @Html.DisplayFor(modelItem => item.Phone)
                    </td>
                </tr>
            }
        </tbody>
    </table>
</div>
```

In this markup, we've applied the `table-striped` and `table-hover` styles to the table. You'll also notice that we've wrapped the column header names inside a `<thead>` element and the table rows inside a `<tbody>` element.

The HTML markup for the view is ready. Complete the following steps to enable the jQuery DataTable functionality for the table:

1. Open the `_Layout.cshtml` file in the `Views\Shared` folder.
2. Add references to the jQuery DataTables base and Bootstrap-specific style sheets by adding the following markup inside the `<head>` element:

   ```
   <link rel="stylesheet" type="text/css" href="//cdn.datatables.net/
   plug-ins/be7019ee387/integration/bootstrap/3/dataTables.bootstrap.
   css">
   <link rel="stylesheet" type="text/css" href="//cdn.datatables.
   net/1.10.0/css/jquery.dataTables.css">
   ```

3. Scroll to the bottom of the `_Layout.cshtml` file and make sure that you have a section declaration for a section called `scripts`:

   ```
   @RenderSection("scripts", required: false)
   ```

4. Open the `Index.cshtml` file in the `Views\Customers` folder. Add the following code to the bottom of the file:

   ```
   @section scripts{
       <script type="text/javascript" language="javascript" src="//
   cdn.datatables.net/1.10.0/js/jquery.dataTables.min.js"></script>
       <script type="text/javascript" language="javascript" src="//
   cdn.datatables.net/plug-ins/be7019ee387/integration/bootstrap/3/
   dataTables.bootstrap.js"></script>
       <script type="text/javascript">
           $(document).ready(function () {
   ```

```
            $('.table').dataTable();
        });
    </script>
}
```

5. In the preceding step, we've added the required references to the DataTables style sheets as well as the JavaScript files. We created a jQuery event handler, which will enable the DataTable functionality on all HTML elements with a class name of `table` as soon as the page loads.

   When you run your project and navigate to the customers view, you'll see that the list of customers are automatically paginated into groups of ten, and you are able to search and sort the data inside the table, as shown in the following screenshot. The default Bootstrap styles for tables are also correctly applied:

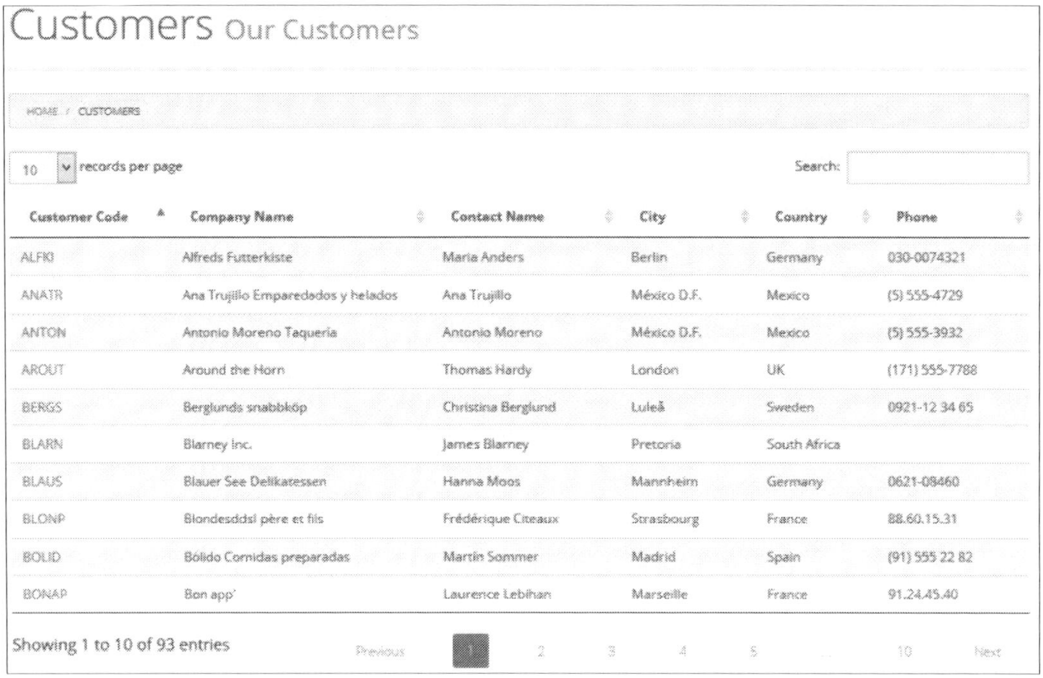

DataTables extensions

The jQuery DataTables plugin provides a wide variety of extensions, which can enhance the functionality of the plugin dramatically.

The ColReorder extension

The ColReorder extension allows users to reorder table columns by clicking-and-dragging the column header to the location they prefer. To enable column reordering for your DataTables HTML table, complete the following steps:

1. Open the `_Layout.cshtml` file and add a reference to the `dataTables.colReorder.css` file:

   ```
   <link rel="stylesheet" type="text/css" href="//cdn.datatables.net/
   colreorder/1.1.1/css/dataTables.colReorder.css">
   ```

2. Open the view `.cshtml` file and add a reference to the DataTables, DataTables Bootstrap, and ColReorder extension JavaScript files:

   ```
   <script type="text/javascript" language="javascript" src="//cdn.
   datatables.net/1.10.0/js/jquery.dataTables.min.js"></script>
   <script type="text/javascript" language="javascript" src="//cdn.
   datatables.net/plug-ins/be7019ee387/integration/bootstrap/3/
   dataTables.bootstrap.js"></script>
   <script type="text/javascript" language="javascript" src="//cdn.
   datatables.net/colreorder/1.1.1/js/dataTables.colReorder.min.
   js"></script>
   ```

3. Lastly, using jQuery, add an event handler to initialize the DataTables plugin and the ColReorder extension after the page has loaded:

   ```
   <script type="text/javascript">
       $(document).ready(function () {
           $('.table').DataTable({
               "dom": 'Rlfrtip'
           });
       });
   </script>
   ```

4. When navigating to the page, you should now be able to drag and reorder the columns in the table. A blue line will be shown when dragging a column, as illustrated in the following screenshot:

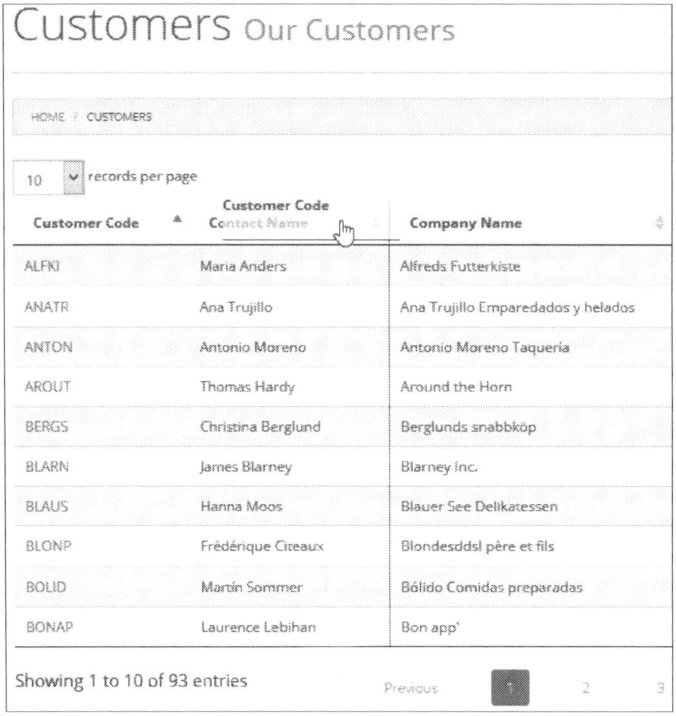

> Notice that we're referencing all the style sheets and JavaScript files for the extensions from the DataTables CDN that are available at `cdn.datatables.net`.

The ColVis extension

The ColVis extension adds a button to the top of DataTable, which when clicked on, displays a list of column names in the table with a checkbox next to it. The user can then deselect the column names they do not wish to see in the grid.

To enable the column visibility extension, perform the following steps:

1. Open the `_Layout.cshtml` file and add a reference to the `dataTables.colVis.css` file:

```
<link rel="stylesheet" type="text/css" href="//cdn.datatables.net/
colvis/1.1.0/css/dataTables.colVis.css">
```

2. Open the view `.cshtml` file and add a reference to the DataTables, DataTables Bootstrap, and ColVis extension JavaScript files:

```
<script type="text/javascript" language="javascript" src="//cdn.
datatables.net/1.10.0/js/jquery.dataTables.min.js"></script>
<script type="text/javascript" language="javascript" src="//cdn.
datatables.net/plug-ins/be7019ee387/integration/bootstrap/3/
dataTables.bootstrap.js"></script>
<script type="text/javascript" language="javascript" src="//cdn.
datatables.net/colvis/1.1.0/js/dataTables.colVis.min.js"></script>
```

3. Lastly, using jQuery, add an event handler to initialize the DataTables plugin and the ColVis extension after the page has loaded:

```
<script type="text/javascript">
    $(document).ready(function () {
        $('.table').DataTable({
            "dom": 'C<"clear">lfrtip'
        });
    });
</script>
```

4. On navigating to the **Customers** page, you should see a button next to the search box with which you can show or hide columns in the table, as shown in the following screenshot:

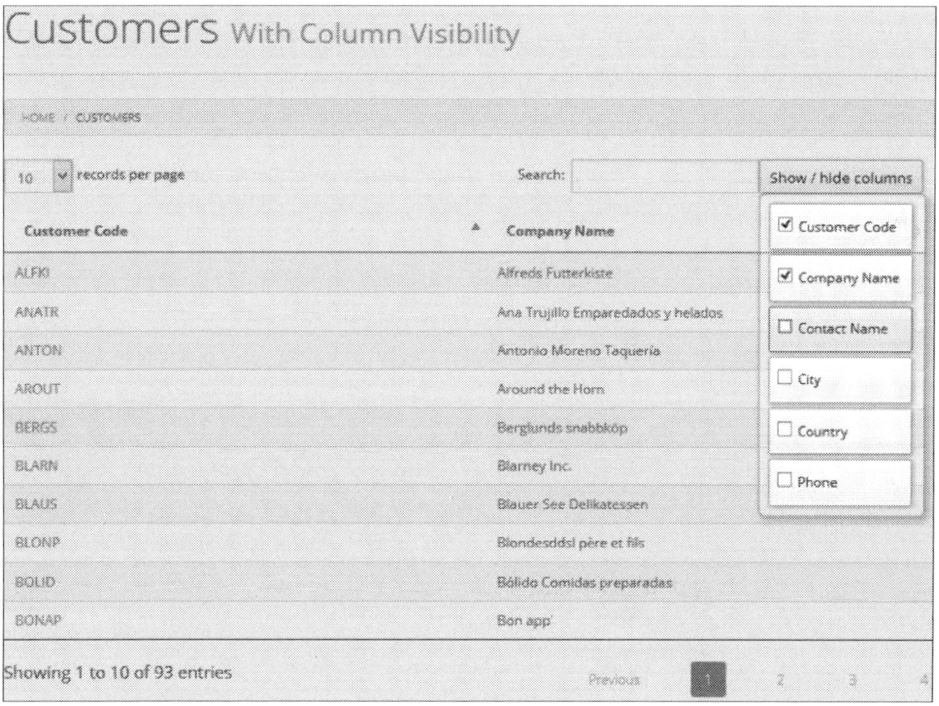

The TableTools extension

The TableTools extension for jQuery DataTables adds a toolbar at the top of the table with which the user can copy to clipboard, export to CSV, and print to PDF the data inside the DataTable. It is a really simple way to give your users the functionality to export their data.

To use the TableTools extension, perform the following steps:

1. Create a new folder in the root of your project called `swf`.
2. Add the `copy_csv_xls_pdf.swf` file to the `swf` folder. The `.swf` file is included in the DataTables plugin download.
3. Open the `_Layout.cshtml` file and add a reference to the `dataTables.tableTools.css` file:

```
<link rel="stylesheet" type="text/css" href="//cdn.datatables.net/tabletools/2.2.1/css/dataTables.tableTools.css">
```

4. Open the view `.cshtml` file and add a reference to the DataTables, DataTables Bootstrap, and TableTools extension JavaScript files:

```
<script type="text/javascript" language="javascript" src="//cdn.datatables.net/1.10.0/js/jquery.dataTables.min.js"></script>
<script type="text/javascript" language="javascript" src="//cdn.datatables.net/tabletools/2.2.1/js/dataTables.tableTools.min.js"></script>
<script type="text/javascript" language="javascript" src="//cdn.datatables.net/plug-ins/be7019ee387/integration/bootstrap/3/dataTables.bootstrap.js"></script>
```

5. Lastly, using jQuery, add an event handler to initialize the DataTables plugin and the TableTools extension after the page has loaded:

```
<script type="text/javascript">
    $(document).ready(function () {
        var table = $('.table').dataTable();
        var tt = new $.fn.dataTable.TableTools(table);
$(tt.fnContainer()).insertBefore('div.dataTables_wrapper');
    });
</script>
```

6. The preceding highlighted code is used to initialize the TableTools extension and to apply Bootstrap styling to the TableTools toolbar buttons. When opening the view with DataTable, you should see a TableTools button toolbar above the DataTable, as shown in the following screenshot:

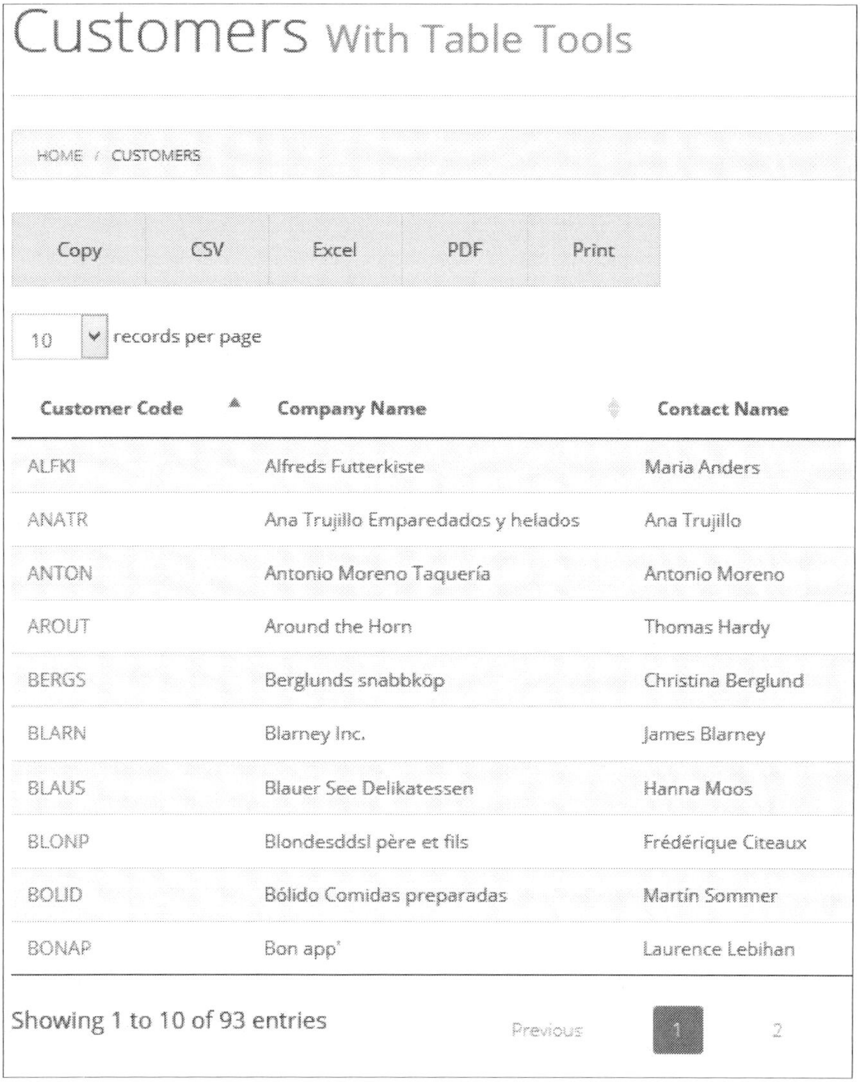

Summary

In this chapter, we've implemented a sortable, searchable, and extensible HTML table using the jQuery DataTables plugin. We also explored how to specify that the plugin should use the default Bootstrap styles. This chapter should also have given you the confidence to explore other open source plugins and incorporate them in your own ASP.NET MVC projects.

In the next and final chapter, we'll take a look at the `TwitterBootstrapMVC` library and how to use it in your own project.

9
Making Things Easier with the TwitterBootstrapMVC Library

The `TwitterBootstrapMVC` library is a fluent implementation of the ASP.NET MVC helpers for Bootstrap. The purpose of this library is to help the ASP.NET MVC developers write any Bootstrap-related HTML markup faster.

We'll explore this library and see how you can include it in your own ASP.NET MVC projects, and how it can help to increase your productivity.

In this chapter, we will cover the following topics:

- What is the `TwitterBootstrapMVC` library and why does it matter
- How to include `TwitterBootstrapMVC` in your project, either through DLL or NuGet
- How to use the `TwitterBootstrapMVC` helpers

The TwitterBootstrapMVC library

The `TwitterBootstrapMVC` library started out as an open source project created by Dmitry Efimenko. The project's goal was to assist developers in creating ASP.NET MVC sites using Bootstrap, by allowing them to use Bootstrap components with fewer lines of code. It can be very time consuming, if you are unfamiliar with the Bootstrap class names, to go through the online documentation on the Bootstrap site. The aim of `TwitterBootstrapMVC` is therefore to simplify website development.

The fluent implementation also provides intelliSense inside Visual Studio, enabling developers to easily discover the Bootstrap configuration options. The library is no longer open source or free, although you can still view the original project on GitHub at `https://github.com/DmitryEfimenko/TwitterBootstrapMvc`.

The commercialized version of the library is available at `https://www.twitterbootstrapmvc.com/`.

Including TwitterBootstrapMVC in your project

You can include the `TwitterBootstrapMVC` library in your project in one of the two ways. The first and preferred option is to use the NuGet package, and the second option is to download and manually add a reference to the `.dll` file.

Adding TwitterBootstrapMVC using NuGet

To include the `TwitterBootstrapMVC` library in your project using NuGet, perform the following steps:

1. In Visual Studio, open the **Package Manager Console** window, via the **Tools | Library Package Manager | Package Manager Console** menu.
2. Inside the **Package Manager console** window, type the following command and hit *Enter*:

   ```
   Install-Package TwitterBootstrapMVC5
   ```

3. Next, navigate to `https://www.twitterbootstrapmvc.com/Download` and download a trial or purchase a personal or commercial license.
4. Download the license file, it should be called `TwitterBootstrapMvcLicense.lic` and add it to the root of your project in Visual Studio.
5. Open the `Web.config` file located inside the `Views` folder and add the following code to the `<namespaces>` element:

   ```
   <add namespace="TwitterBootstrapMVC" />
   <add namespace="TwitterBootstrap3" />
   ```

6. Finally, open the `Global.asax` file in the root of your project and add the following line of code to the `Application_Start` method:

   ```
   Bootstrap.Configure();
   ```

Add TwitterBootstrapMVC using the .dll file

You do not need to add the `TwitterBootstrapMVC` library via NuGet, you can also add it using the `.dll` file. To do this, complete the following steps:

1. Inside your browser, navigate to `https://www.twitterbootstrapmvc.com/Home/Installation` and download the zip archive located under the **Option 2: Download a .dll** heading.
2. After the zip file has been downloaded, extract the files to a folder on a local drive.
3. Inside Visual Studio, right-click on the **References** node in the **Solution Explorer** window and select **Add Reference...** from the context menu.
4. Browse to the folder where you've extracted the zip archive and select the `TwitterBootstrapMVC5.dll` file.
5. Next, navigate to `https://www.twitterbootstrapmvc.com/Download` and download a trial or purchase a personal or commercial license.
6. Download the license file, it should be called `TwitterBootstrapMvcLicense.lic` and add it to the root of your project in Visual Studio.
7. Open the `Web.config` file located inside the `Views` folder and add the following code to the `<namespaces>` element:

   ```
   <add namespace="TwitterBootstrapMVC" />
   <add namespace="TwitterBootstrap3" />
   ```

8. Finally, open the `Global.asax` file in the root of your project and add the following line of code to the `Application_Start` method:

   ```
   Bootstrap.Configure();
   ```

Using the TwitterBootstrapMVC helpers

The `TwitterBootstrapMVC` library offers a wide range of Bootstrap helpers, all of whom use a fluent syntax to allow the chaining of methods. These helpers can reduce the amount of HTML markup you need to create the Bootstrap components. Method chaining in the library follows the following pattern:

```
@Html.Bootstrap().TextBoxFor(m => m.PostalCode).Value("1.23").
Size(InputSize.Large).Placeholder("Enter Postal Code").
Format("{0:0.00}").Prepend("US")
```

Forms and inputs

`TwitterBootstrapMVC` offers fluent helpers for most forms and input elements.

Inputs

`TwitterBootstrapMVC` supplies ASP.NET MVC helpers for all HTML input elements; most of these components share the same chaining methods. These methods are listed in the following table:

Method name	Description
`.Label()`	This prepends a `label` element to the element
`.Tooltip()`	This adds a tooltip to the component with the supplied message
`.HelpText()`	This adds a helper text next to the element
`.Id()`	This sets the `id` attribute of the element
`.Class()`	This sets the `class` HTML attribute of the element
`.ReadOnly()`	This adds `readonly="readonly"` to the element
`.HtmlAttributes()`	This adds the specified HTML attribute(s) to the element
`.Data()`	This works in a similar fashion as the `.HtmlAttributes()` method but prepends `data-` to the attribute
`.Disabled()`	This adds `disabled="disabled"` to the element
`.DisabledDependsOn()`	This disables an element that is conditionally based on the value of another element
`.VisibleDependsOn()`	This hides an element that is conditionally based on the value of another element
`.ShowValidationMessage()`	This sets whether the validation message should be shown for an element in case its validation fails

Forms

Using the following code, you can generate a simple vertical Bootstrap form containing three textboxes and a `submit` button. The first two textboxes also invoke the `PlaceHolder` method that adds the placeholder text to the empty textboxes and the last textbox has an additional method called `HelpText` that adds the helper text to the bottom of the textbox.

```
@using (var form = Html.Bootstrap().Begin(new Form()))
{
    @form.FormGroup().TextBoxFor(m => m.CompanyName).
    Placeholder("Enter the company name.")
    @form.FormGroup().TextBoxFor(m => m.ContactName).
    Placeholder("Enter the name of contact person.")
    @form.FormGroup().TextBoxFor(m => m.Address).HelpText
    ("Short address for customer.")
    @Html.Bootstrap().SubmitButton()
}
```

The resulting form should look similar to the following screenshot in the browser:

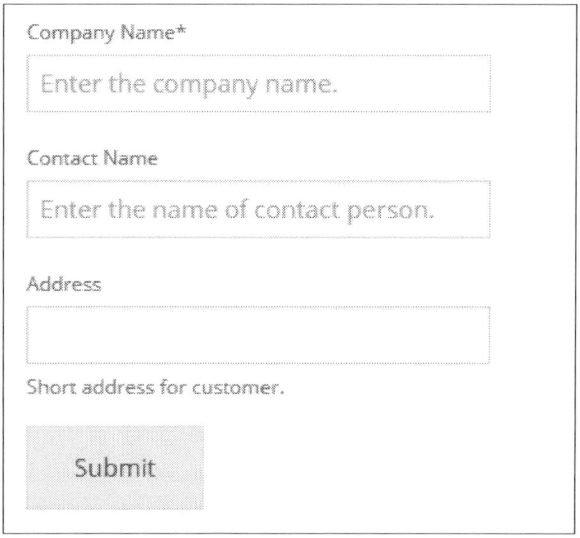

You'll also notice that the `FormGroup` helper is smart enough to automatically add an asterisk (`*`) to the fields' label, if the value is required.

To generate the same form as an inline or vertical form is as simple as invoking the `Type` method on the `Form` object and specifying the layout as a parameter to the `Type` method. The parameter is an enumeration (`enum`) value, which enables intelliSense that lists all the available options:

```
@using (var form = Html.Bootstrap().Begin(new Form().Type(FormType.
Inline)))
{
    @form.FormGroup().TextBoxFor(m => m.CompanyName).
    Placeholder("Enter the company name.")
    @form.FormGroup().TextBoxFor(m => m.ContactName).
    Placeholder("Enter the name of contact person.")
    @form.FormGroup().TextBoxFor(m => m.Address)
    @Html.Bootstrap().SubmitButton()
}
```

The resulting form will appear similar to the following screenshot:

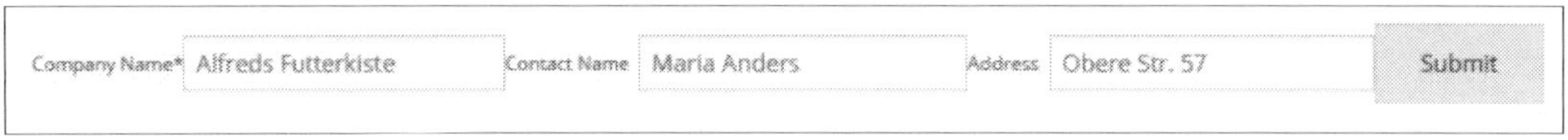

The `Textbox` helper offers the following extension methods to add additional formatting or functionality to a `textbox` element:

Method name	Description
`.Value()`	This sets the value of the textbox.
`.Size()`	This sets the size of the textbox. This also accepts the `Inputsize` enum.
`.Placeholder()`	This specifies the placeholder text of the textbox.
`.Format()`	This is used to specify the data format of the textbox.
`.Append()`	This appends the specified string to the end of the textbox. This also creates an input group.
`.AppendIcon()`	This appends an icon to the end of the textbox.
`.Prepend()`	This is the opposite of the `.Append()` method. This adds the specified string to the front of the textbox and also creates an input group.
`.PrependIcon()`	This adds the specified icon to the front of the textbox.
`.TypeAhead()`	This enables the `TypeAhead` functionality for the textbox.

In the following example, we'll create a textbox for the models' `PostalCode` property, set its `value` element to `1.23`, and its `size` to `Large`. We'll then specify the placeholder text and the format, and finally, we add a string to the front of the textbox:

```
@Html.Bootstrap().TextBoxFor(m => m.MinimumTransactionValue).
Value("1.23").Size(InputSize.Large).Placeholder("Enter Postal Code").
Format("{0:0.00}").Prepend("US")
```

The resulting textbox should look similar to the following screenshot in your browser:

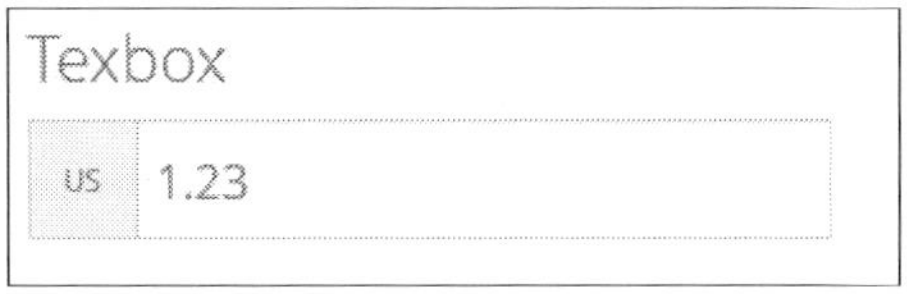

To create a text area input using the `TwitterBootstrapMVC` library, you can use the `TextAreaFor` helper. This helper supports two additional methods with which you can specify the number of columns and rows for the text area. In the following example, we'll create a text area for the models' `Address` property and set its `columns` value to `10` and its `rows` value to `5`:

```
@Html.Bootstrap().TextAreaFor(m => m.Address).Columns(10).Rows(5)
```

The text areas should be rendered similar to the following screenshot in your browser:

Buttons and links

The `TwitterBootstrapMVC` library provides fluent helpers for Bootstrap buttons as well as links. Both buttons and links helpers share the following extension methods:

Method name	Description
`.AppendIcon()`	This appends the specified icon to the button or link
`.PrependIcon()`	This prepends the specified icon to the button or link
`.Disabled()`	This adds the `disabled` class to the button or link

In the following code example, we'll create a simple `submit` button that has an icon at the back and at the front of it. Note the use of the `glyphicon` class names in order to specify which icons to use.

```
@Html.Bootstrap().Button().AppendIcon("glyphicon glyphicon-pencil").
PrependIcon("glyphicon glyphicon-music")
```

The preceding markup will render the following screenshot in your browser:

The `ActionLinkButton`, `Button`, and `SubmitButton` helpers share the following extension methods:

Method name	Description
`.Text()`	This sets the caption/text of the button.
`.Name()`	This specifies the HTML `name` attribute.
`.Value()`	This sets the `value` HTML attribute.
`.Size()`	This specifies the size of the button. This also accepts the `ButtonSize` enum as a parameter.
`.Style()`	This sets the style of the button. This also accepts the `ButtonStyle` enum as a parameter.
`.ButtonBlock()`	This expands the button to the full width of the container.

Method name	Description
`.LoadingText()`	This sets the text that should be displayed after the button was clicked.
`.DropDownToggle()`	This applies the `dropdown-toggle` class name to the button.

The following code generates a large, green Bootstrap button and sets its caption using the `TwitterBootstrapMVC` fluent helper syntax:

```
@Html.Bootstrap().Button().Text("Buy Now").Size(ButtonSize.Large).
Style(ButtonStyle.Success)
```

The button will resemble the following screenshot in your browser:

The `ActionLinkButton` and `ActionLink` helpers share the following extension methods:

Method name	Description
`.Protocol()`	This specifies the URL's protocol, for example, `http` or `https`
`.HostName()`	This sets the hostname of the URL
`.Fragment()`	This sets the anchor name of the URL
`.RouteName()`	This specifies the route name
`.RouteValues()`	This sets the route values
`.Title()`	This sets the `title` HTML attribute

In the following code, we'll create an `ActionLinkButton` object. Note how we combined the `.Style` and `.PrependIcons` methods with the `ActionLinkButton` method:

```
@Html.Bootstrap().ActionLinkButton("Go to Buttons", "Buttons").
Protocol("http").Title("Buttons Link").Style(ButtonStyle.Link).
PrependIcon("glyphicon glyphicon-film")
```

The result will be a link with an icon rendered inside your browser, as shown in the following screenshot:

Accordions and panels

Both the `accordion` and `panel` helpers, which `TwitterBootstrapMVC` provides, should be used with the disposable `Begin` method.

The `accordion` method has another method called `BeginPanel`, which is used to indicate a new panel inside the `accordion` component. The following code will generate an accordion with two panels. Note that both panels are also disposable.

```
@using (var accordian = Html.Bootstrap().Begin(new Accordion("FAQ")))
{
    using (accordian.BeginPanel("Question 1"))
    {
        <p>tiam luctus nunc ipsum, sed facilisis velit.<p>
    }
    using (accordian.BeginPanel("Question 2"))
    {
        <p>Duis volutpat iaculis nisl, ut porttitor.<p>
    }
}
```

The accordion should look similar to the following screenshot in your browser:

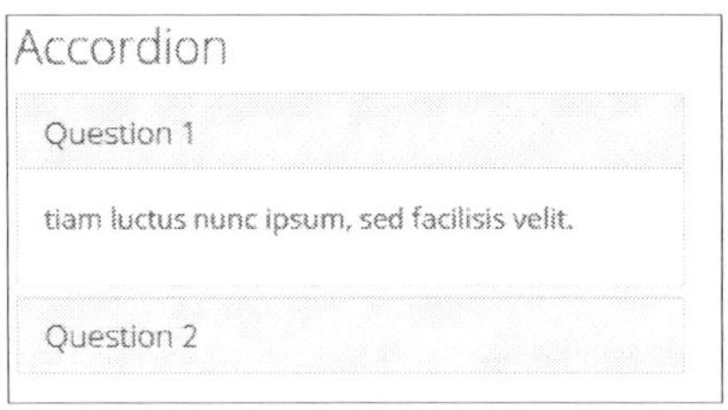

The `panel` helper includes three child methods, `BeginHeading`, `BeginBody`, and `BeginFooter`. These methods can also be invoked by using a shorthand notation by invoking either the `Heading`, `Body`, or `Footer` methods.

Using the following code, we'll generate a panel with a heading and footer. We'll also specify the style of the panel by calling the shared `Style` method on the `Panel` object.

```
@using (var panel = Html.Bootstrap().Begin(new Panel().
Style(PanelStyle.Danger)))
{
    @panel.Heading("Panel Heading")

    using (panel.BeginBody())
    {
        <p>Proin mattis lacus ac enim aliquam, eu malesuada
        tortor pretium.</p>
    }
    @panel.Footer("Panel Footer")
}
```

This code will render the following screenshot in your browser:

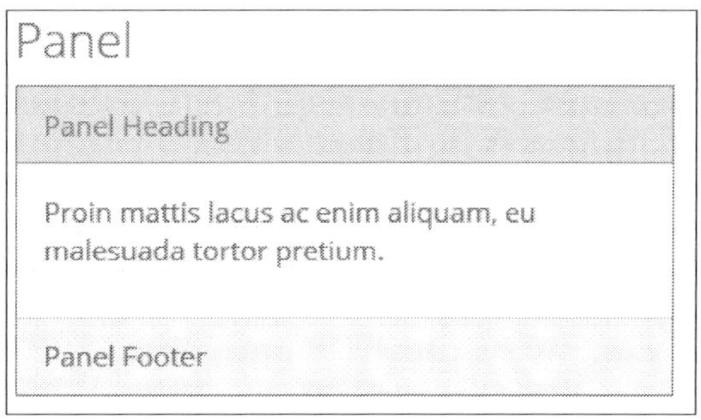

Tabs and modals

Fluent helpers are also available for the `tab` and `modal` components. A new `tab` component should be created using the disposable `Begin` method. Each tab inside the `tab` component must be declared using the `Tab` extension method and the content of each tab should reside inside the `BeginPanel` method.

In the following example, we'll create a `tab` component with two tabs. Note the use of the `AppendBadge` extension method on the `Tab` method.

```
@using (var tabs = Html.Bootstrap().Begin(new Tabs("TabComponent")))
{
    @tabs.Tab("Tab One")
```

```
        @tabs.Tab("Tab Two").AppendBadge("10")

        using (tabs.BeginPanel())
        {
            <p>Tab One content</p>
        }
        using (tabs.BeginPanel())
        {
            <p>Tab Two Content</p>
        }
    }
```

This markup results in the following screenshot in your browser:

The `Modal` class has the following methods:

Method name	Description
`.Closeable()`	This adds a `close` button to the modal header
`.BackdropOff()`	This will cause the modal to close only when its `close` button is clicked
`.FadeOff()`	This removes the fade effect
`.KeyboardOff()`	This prevents the modal from being closed when the *Esc* key is pressed
`.Remote()`	This specifies that the modal content should be loaded via Ajax from the specified path
`.ShowOff()`	This prevents the modal from being shown when it was initialized

The following code will create a button that will show a modal with the ID that was specified as parameter to the `TriggerModal` method once it is clicked on. The `Modal` object is declared using the disposable `Begin` method in conjunction with the `Modal` class. The heading is created using the `Header` method and the body content is contained inside the `BeginBody` method.

```
@Html.Bootstrap().Button().Text("Show Modal").TriggerModal("myModal")
@using (var modal = Html.Bootstrap().Begin(new Modal().Id("myModal")))
{
    @modal.Header("Modal Heading")
    using (modal.BeginBody())
    {
        <p>Aliquam porttitor faucibus lectus, quis hendrerit
        orci scelerisque sit amet. Cras est augue.</p>
        <p>Aliquam imperdiet nibh eget libero rutrum sodales. </p>
    }
    using (modal.BeginFooter())
    {
        @Html.Bootstrap().Button().Text("Close").Style
       (ButtonStyle.Info);
    }
}
```

The result should be a modal dialog with a blue info Bootstrap button as the modal close button, as shown in the following screenshot:

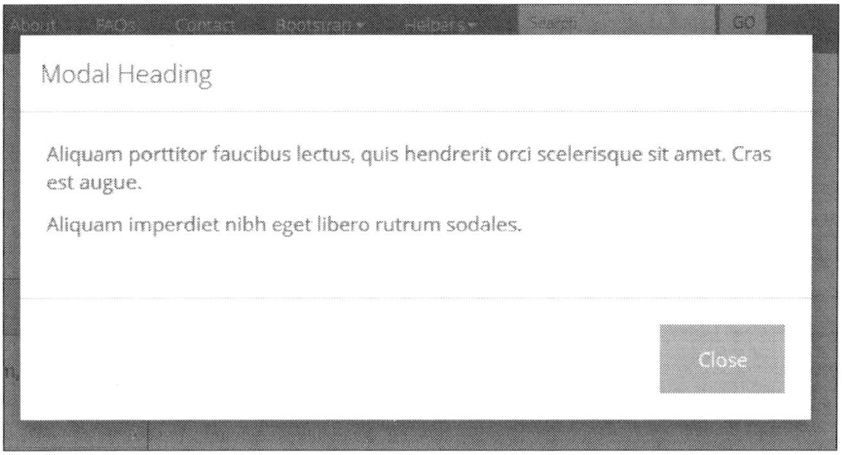

Summary

In this chapter, you were introduced to the `TwitterBootstrapMVC` library and saw how you can reduce the amount of markup of your views using this library. This is also the last chapter of this book, and by now, you should be fairly comfortable with using Bootstrap in your own ASP.NET MVC projects and even be ready to write your own code-generation tools and helpers.

Make sure you download the sample project that accompanies this book from the Packt Publishing website to see the examples mentioned in this book in action.

Thank you for reading. Until next time, keep coding!

Bootstrap Resources

The Bootstrap community is a vibrant and vast one. The following sections, in no particular order, are a list of Bootstrap resources available on the Internet.

Themes

The URLs for downloading free and premium HTML themes based on Bootstrap are listed in the following table:

URL	Description
`http://startbootstrap.com/`	This URL provides free HTML starter templates and themes for Bootstrap.
`https://wrapbootstrap.com/`	This is a marketplace for premium themes and templates for Bootstrap.
`http://bit.ly/ThemeForestHtml`	ThemeForest has over 5,000 premium HTML templates. Many of them are based on Bootstrap.
`http://www.prepbootstrap.com/`	This URL provides free Bootstrap themes, templates, and other widgets with complete code examples.
`http://bootstrapzero.com/`	This URL provides open source Bootstrap themes and templates.
`http://bootswatch.com/`	This URL provides free themes for Bootstrap.

Add-ons

The URLs for additional add-ons, plugins, and components for Bootstrap are listed in the following table:

URL	Description
`http://bit.ly/FuelUX`	FuelUX provides additional controls and enhancements for Bootstrap such as date pickers, spinners, trees, and form wizards.
`http://bit.ly/JasnyBootstrap`	Jasny Bootstrap provides some enhancements to existing components such as label buttons and anchored alerts.
`http://bit.ly/BootstrapNotify`	Bootstrap notify makes it easier to display alert style notifications to your users.
`http://bootstrapformhelpers.com/`	Bootstrap Form Helpers is a plugin to help enhance your forms. It includes color pickers, sliders, and so on.
`http://www.bootstrap-switch.org/`	This add-on turn your checkboxes into iOS-style switch controls.
`http://bit.ly/BSAppWiz`	This add-on adds multistep, wizard-like interfaces to your forms with the Bootstrap Application Wizard.
`http://tableclothjs.com/`	This add-on makes your Bootstrap tables sortable and searchable using jQuery.
`http://bit.ly/TypeAhead`	This add-on provides a plugin by Twitter. This also adds the autocomplete feature to your forms.

Editors and generators

The URLs for tools to help you design and build your Bootstrap site are listed in the following table:

URL	Description
`http://www.bootstrapbundle.com/`	This URL provides an ASP.NET MVC Bootstrap project and item templates for Visual Studio 2013.
`http://www.layoutit.com/`	This URL provides the drag-and-drop interface builder for Bootstrap.

URL	Description
`https://www.easel.io/`	This is similar to LayoutIt. It provides a visual drag-and-drop interface to build your Bootstrap UI.
`https://jetstrap.com/`	This URL provides a visual interface building tool for Bootstrap.
`http://www.bootply.com/`	This URL provides a visual editor for rapidly building interfaces for Bootstrap.
`http://www.divshot.com/`	This URL provides Bootstrap builder and static web hosting tools.
`http://bit.ly/BSMagic`	Bootstrap Magic easily creates your own theme for Bootstrap.
`http://paintstrap.com/`	This URL provides a tool to generate Bootstrap themes using a COLOURlovers color scheme.
`http://www.bootstrapdesigner.com/`	This URL provides a tool to generate websites or templates for Bootstrap.

Index

Symbols

A

B

C

D

E

F

G

H

I

J

L

M

N

P

S

T

V

[PACKT] open source
community experience distilled
PUBLISHING

Thank you for buying
Bootstrap for ASP.NET MVC

About Packt Publishing

Packt, pronounced 'packed', published its first book "*Mastering phpMyAdmin for Effective MySQL Management*" in April 2004 and subsequently continued to specialize in publishing highly focused books on specific technologies and solutions.

Our books and publications share the experiences of your fellow IT professionals in adapting and customizing today's systems, applications, and frameworks. Our solution based books give you the knowledge and power to customize the software and technologies you're using to get the job done. Packt books are more specific and less general than the IT books you have seen in the past. Our unique business model allows us to bring you more focused information, giving you more of what you need to know, and less of what you don't.

Packt is a modern, yet unique publishing company, which focuses on producing quality, cutting-edge books for communities of developers, administrators, and newbies alike. For more information, please visit our website: `www.packtpub.com`.

About Packt Open Source

In 2010, Packt launched two new brands, Packt Open Source and Packt Enterprise, in order to continue its focus on specialization. This book is part of the Packt Open Source brand, home to books published on software built around Open Source licenses, and offering information to anybody from advanced developers to budding web designers. The Open Source brand also runs Packt's Open Source Royalty Scheme, by which Packt gives a royalty to each Open Source project about whose software a book is sold.

Writing for Packt

We welcome all inquiries from people who are interested in authoring. Book proposals should be sent to `author@packtpub.com`. If your book idea is still at an early stage and you would like to discuss it first before writing a formal book proposal, contact us; one of our commissioning editors will get in touch with you.

We're not just looking for published authors; if you have strong technical skills but no writing experience, our experienced editors can help you develop a writing career, or simply get some additional reward for your expertise.

[PACKT] open source
community experience distilled
PUBLISHING

Bootstrap Site Blueprints

ISBN: 978-1-78216-452-4 Paperback: 304 pages

Design mobile-first responsive websites with Bootstrap 3

1. Learn the inner working of Bootstrap 3 and create web applications with ease.
2. Quickly customize your designs working directly with Bootstrap's LESS files.
3. Leverage Bootstrap's excellent JavaScript plugins.

Extending Bootstrap

ISBN: 978-1-78216-841-6 Paperback: 88 pages

Understand Bootstrap and unlock its secrets to build a truly customized project!

1. Learn to use themes to improve your user experience.
2. Improve your workflow with LESS and Grunt.js.
3. Get to know the most useful third- party Bootstrap plugins.

Please check **www.PacktPub.com** for information on our titles